Using Your Sociological Imagination: Thinking and Writing Critically

A Workbook

to accompany

Sociology in a Changing World

THIRD EDITION

WILLIAM KORNBLUM

and

CAROLYN D. SMITH

Harcourt Brace College Publishers

Fort Worth   Philadelphia   San Diego   New York   Orlando   Austin   San Antonio
Toronto   Montreal   London   Sydney   Tokyo

ISBN: 0-15-501433-1

Address for editorial correspondence: Harcourt Brace College Publishers, 301 Commerce Street,
Suite 3700, Fort Worth, TX 76102

Address for orders: Harcourt Brace & Company, 6277 Sea Harbor Drive, Orlando, Florida 32887.
1-800-782-4479, or 1-800-433-0001 (in Florida)

PRINTED IN THE UNITED STATES OF AMERICA

5 6 7 8 9 0 1 2   095   9 8 7 6 5 4

INTRODUCTION

Using Your Sociological Imagination: Thinking and Writing Critically is a workbook designed to accompany the third edition of *Sociology in a Changing World*, by William Kornblum. Each chapter of the workbook contains six exercises whose purpose is to encourage you to think carefully about what you have learned in the corresponding chapter of the text. Several types of questions are included. Some require that you evaluate a recent event from a sociological perspective; some ask you to refer to a table or chart in the text; some encourage you to think critically about concepts discussed in the text. One exercise in each chapter is based on the Critical Response at the end of the chapter summary.

The workbook exercises may be assigned as homework to be submitted. But even if they are not, it will be worthwhile to complete each set of exercises after reading the corresponding chapter of the text. This workbook will provide an opportunity not only to apply what you have learned but also to practice the skills needed to answer essay questions on examinations.

BUILDING CRITICAL THINKING AND WRITING SKILLS

Good writing is a key to success in college. It can also be the secret of success in many occupations and professions such as law, science, and business. But what is good writing? And why is there so much emphasis on writing these days? The answer to the second question is easy: Along with the rapid expansion of the store of knowledge has come a growing need for people who can organize knowledge and write about it in ways that others will understand. But the first question is much harder to answer. There are many definitions of good writing, just as there are many kinds of writing. Here we will be dealing with several aspects of good writing, with emphasis on writing in the social sciences.

Perhaps the most important feature of strong writing is that it is clear and direct and comes to the point in every paragraph. In good writing, the author knows what he or she is trying to say in every sentence. To achieve this goal, one needs to be extremely critical of one's own ideas and the way they are organized, which is why critical thinking skills are so important to good writing. To be a good writer one must learn to ask critical questions about what one reads, to find weaknesses in arguments and expose fuzzy thinking—especially one's own.

Writing and Critical Thinking

In the social sciences we are constantly confronted with "received wisdoms"—ideas that people tend to believe without using their critical abilities to question them. Prejudices and commonsense assumptions about social life are among the received wisdoms that are especially damaging to efforts to think logically and scientifically about the social world. When one hears statements such as "There will always be some people who are selfish" or "It's human nature that causes crime" or "People on welfare just don't want to work," these are personal beliefs or prejudices that may or may not be accurate in the situation to which they are being applied. When stated repeatedly with no attempt to question their truth, they are the opposite of critical thought. And when used in sociological writing, they can lead to harsh criticism (and low grades).

But simple acceptance of received wisdoms is only one kind of uncritical thought. On a more sophisticated level, we find received wisdoms that serve as single explanations of social life. Extreme radicals, for example, may seek to explain all social problems as resulting from class conflict. Ultra-conservatives, on the other hand, may explain social problems of all kinds as resulting from excess governmental interference. These are single ideas that one often hears used to explain situations that actually require more diverse and subtle explanations. Unless one is critical of such single explanations, one cannot write well about social life.

In thinking critically, it is helpful to ask a series of questions about any idea or statement: What is the point being made? Is that point supported by the facts? Can I think of instances in which it would not be justified? Does this point lead logically to other points in the argument in which it is presented? Does the point reflect a bias or prejudice or self-serving attitude on the part of its originator?

Written statements demand the same critical thought, no matter how famous their author is said to be. Written statements should also be subjected to a series of questions about the writing itself: Do the sentences make sense? Can they be simplified without doing harm to their meaning, and if so, why were they so long and complicated in the first place? On the other hand, are they too short and oversimplified? If so, does this mean that the writer has not given enough thought to the subject?

In a famous criticism of what he called Grand Theory, C. Wright Mills took aim at sociologists who write long, abstract passages of social theory. Here is an example of such a passage, followed by Mills's translation:

> Attachment to common values means, motivationally considered, that the actors have common "sentiments" in support of the value patterns, which may be treated as a "good thing" relatively independently of any specific instrumental "advantage" to be gained from such conformity, e.g., in

the avoidance of negative sanctions. Furthermore, this attachment to common values, while it may fit the immediate gratificational needs of the actor, always has also a "moral" aspect in that to some degree this conformity defines the "responsibilities" of the actor in the wider, that is, social action systems in which he participates.

(from Talcott Parsons, *The Social System*)

When people share the same values, they tend to behave in accordance with the way they expect one another to behave. Moreover, they often treat such conformity as a very good thing—even when it seems to go against their immediate interests.

(Mills, 1959, p. 31)

By simplifying the dense writing in the first paragraph, Mills is trying to render it more intelligible to any reader. He is also trying to get to the points buried in the convoluted sentences so that their value can be assessed critically. This kind of critical thinking must be applied to ideas and statements, both those of others and one's own, if one is to write with strength and clarity.

Writing Assignments in Sociology Courses

Although the elements of good writing are the same no matter what the assignment, there are important differences in what one can be expected to produce in different kinds of writing assignments. Following are some suggestions for organizing and writing the most common types of written assignments in sociology courses: essay questions on exams, short themes, reading notes, and research papers.

Essay Questions. These are usually written in the student's handwriting in an exam booklet, known in many colleges and universities as a "blue book," under conditions of rather intense time pressure. These conditions tend to produce a good deal of anxiety, which is often reflected in poor-quality writing.

In fact, however, once a student has thought about what the instructor is looking for in a question, and about how to organize the answer, it is relatively easy to write a good essay. Here is a description of the process one might follow in answering an essay question like this one:

Distinguish between role conflict and role strain, giving examples of each. Why do you think role conflicts are more likely to occur in more complex societies than in simpler ones?

Before launching into the written answer, write an outline in schematic form. This outline will give you a structure and show the instructor what you were thinking about in preparing to write the answer. Try to stay with the outline as you do the actual writing. The more detailed and specific you have made the outline, the easier it will be to stay with it.

In the first paragraph or two of your answer, present the broadest idea needed to develop the essay. In our example, it would be a definition of what a role is and how it organizes important aspects of human behavior. Any time you define a term, using your own language or that of an authority, always try to offer an example that makes the definition concrete. Unless you show that you understand the concept of a role—that it is the behavior associated with a status in society—it will be difficult to go on to role conflict and role strain.

In the next section of the essay, write paragraphs that define role conflict and role strain. Again, be sure to provide examples. End this section with a brief paragraph that explains the difference between the two concepts. The last section of the essay must answer the second part of the question, which asks why role conflicts are more likely to appear in complex societies than in simpler ones. The answer deals with the greater number of roles that people in complex societies carry out; for example, a woman is typically a student, a mother, a worker, a committee member, and so on— a far greater number of roles than she would have in a traditional village society. The likelihood that these roles will demand behaviors that are incompatible, such as staying home with children and going to work in an office, is quite great. In a village society a woman is also a mother and a worker, but the roles are combined; her work in the fields is close by and her children are typically there with her, so the potential for conflict is less than it is when her roles require her to be in different places.

This was a rather simple essay to outline, especially since the major sections are suggested by the questions posed, which is not at all uncommon for essay exams. It is important to make sure you answer each of the questions and include a paragraph or section corresponding to each part of the overall essay question.

When you have finished writing your essay, *read it over and correct any obvious mistakes.* Essay questions in sociology are not typically judged on the basis of writing style or grammatical correctness, but you should get in the habit of always reading over what you have written. Take pride in your writing and polish it wherever possible. Corrections on an essay are acceptable; they show the instructor that you care. These are small touches that reveal a great deal about you as a student and future professional.

The Short Theme. This is usually a short piece of writing, about two or three pages, designed to test your ability to organize thoughts into a coherent argument or description. The question may be quite broad, such as "Describe how social change affects your own life." But such questions can usually be narrowed down. Social change involves changes occurring throughout society, but only those that impinge on your own life count in this assignment. Choose some examples and develop them into a coherent statement. Always use whole paragraphs and complete sentences.

Normally one begins academic writing assignments with an organizing paragraph that states the issue or theme and in three or four sentences explains how one will approach the problem or develop the theme. But it is always worthwhile to try for some innovation in the opening paragraph. A short vignette—that is, a brief story about how a specific change has altered your life or your immediate social world—would grab the reader's attention. From the vignette you can proceed to a more general statement of what the issues are, in this case how the events in the opening example are characteristic of larger-scale changes affecting others as well. This approach would make for an effective organizing strategy.

A short theme is an opportunity to try out some writing techniques, to be daring. But this does not mean that you need to labor long hours to construct "deep" thoughts or produce a smashing sentence. In fact, you should avoid sentences such as this one: "Social change affects my life in myriad ways, from the sublime to the ridiculous, from the mundane to the tragic, from the macro to the micro levels of my life." This is an example of what is often called "purple prose"; it is full of superficially impressive sounds and inflated claims but does not carry much meaning at all. What are the myriad ways? What social changes does the writer have in mind? This sentence sounds like a student trying out a mixture of sociological terms, such as *micro* and *macro levels,* and some literary ones, such as *tragedy* and *sublime.* A clearer sentence would be one such as this: "Social change affects every aspect of my life, from the most minor aspects of my behavior at home to the plans I have for the future." Then you would go on to explain what this sentence suggests by first dealing with the small-scale, micro-level changes and then describing the larger ones that affect your future. If you work your feelings into the writing through adjectives and statements about how you feel about the changes in your life, your essay will gain power without the need for any purple prose.

Reading Notes. These are often a precursor to a research paper. They demonstrate the kind of data or supporting material that you have been finding to use in the longer paper. Also, when students are involved in any professional field work for researchers they are often asked to prepare reading notes or to summarize literature. This assignment is therefore particularly useful in that it has direct applications to professional research and writing.

Reading notes must provide all the required bibliographic information at the top of the page where the entry begins. If you have never done a research bibliography or do not remember how to set down the information, consult a writer's manual such as the *Harbrace College Handbook* or *A Manual for Writers,* by Kate Turabian (published by the University of Chicago Press). Summarize what you have read and indicate whether it is a partial reading of a longer work by including the author's central problem or theme, the kinds of evidence he or she uses (for example, if it is an empirical study, make sure you briefly summarize what data were collected and when the original research was done; if it is a historical work, note the types of historical information included in the book, paper, and so on), and the conclusions or recommendations the author draws from the research. If you are looking for a specific argument or type of information and the reading does not have it, you should mention that as well. You can get a good idea about what goes into reading notes on research papers by consulting *Sociological Abstracts,* which provide up-to-date information about scholarly papers in all the subfields of sociology. For longer books you will want to write a note on each chapter or on the chapters that apply most directly to your project.

The Research Paper. This project is usually rather ambitious and may extend over an entire semester. An honors thesis may be a year-long project. The research papers one writes in college are a way of learning how to approach the research and writing one may do later when carrying out professional assignments—legal briefs, scientific papers, theses, prospectuses, and the like.

In the case of a one-semester research paper, it is a good idea to get started on the assignment as soon as possible. We all have had the experience of trying to "get over" at the end of a semester. It can be done, but usually with mediocre results and an unimpressive grade. You will be surprised to see how much you can accomplish with relative ease by the end of the semester if you follow a few simple guidelines: Choose a topic immediately, stick to it, and work on the project each week according to a planned schedule of *background research, brainstorming* and *note taking, thesis development* and *outlining, drafting,* and *rewriting.* Some of these phases can be undertaken simultaneously, but others clearly must await the completion of prior tasks.

Suppose, for example, that the topic of your sociology research paper is date rape, an issue about which a great deal of information is available in recent studies and articles, and one that raises larger issues of social criticism and social theory. First realize that you have a subject, or *topic,* not a thesis or argument or viewpoint. Date rape is a topic. The idea that the increase in reported incidents of date rape is explained by women's greater willingness to come forward about it is the beginning of a *thesis,* an argument that one could explore through research. It is important to move quickly from the broad topic of date rape to a more focused thesis. You may have strong feelings about the topic, and these can be helpful in framing your argument, but you must be careful that your own bias does not prevent you from learning from the research. It is not what you believed before doing the research that matters, but what you allow yourself to learn through the research itself.

Brainstorming is a process in which you think of as many ideas and issues that bear on the topic as possible. Sometimes it is worthwhile to brainstorm with friends, who will come up with other ideas and associations about the subject. The reading notes you prepare about articles and books on the subject will later serve as paragraphs or parts of paragraphs in your paper. But they can serve you well only if they are done well from the start. They should be legibly written or typed, with a few cogent quotations about important points that you may want to include in your paper.

The sources you use should represent solid contributions to the literature. For a sociology paper it is best to consult sociological journals and other sources. Start with *Sociological Abstracts,* the *American Journal of Sociology,* and *Society* magazine. Other sources will appear in the bibliographies of the articles you read. Finally, in gathering the sources for your paper be aware of what kinds of evidence best support the kind of argument you are making. If the issues are quantitative, involving increases or decreases in social phenomena, try to marshal at least some quantitative indicators of what it is you are studying or trying to show. Numerical tables or graphs can be extremely valuable in such presentations.

For a more theoretical argument you will need to present the ideas of many different commentators and theorists. In that case it is important to know how to use quotations, to be careful in selecting the best and most succinct ones, and to know how to paraphrase ideas in your own words. Make sure that whenever you are using other people's words you cite the source, including the page on which the quoted material appears. Even when you are using an idea from another source or a fact stated in your own words, try to show what sources you used to make the statement. Always do so. Failure to document can lead you into plagiarism. To cite carefully is to demonstrate how much research you have done.

In constructing the outline for your first draft, put a good deal of thought into what the major sections of the paper will be and how they will be titled. Try to use section titles that convey meaning and help the reader know what you are saying in the section. For example, a beginning section titled "Introduction" is not very helpful. A title such as "The Date Rape Controversy: An Overview" is somewhat longer and carries valuable information. It is extremely useful to provide a brief summary paragraph at the end of each section of the paper, ending with a transition that will prepare the reader for what is coming next. For example: "This introduction has presented the basic terms of the debate over this growing social problem. The scholarly literature on the subject offers additional insight into the recent research on the scope and explanations of date rape." This transition clearly indicates that the next section of the paper will discuss issues that you have identified in your literature review.

"Say what you are going to do, do it, and say what you have done." So goes an old rule of essay and term paper organization. This rule is mainly a caution not to hold your best ideas, findings, or recommendations until the end of the paper because your fickle reader may never get there. Put your main points or findings in the introduction and spend the remainder of the paper elaborating on them. End by summarizing why they are your main points, and you will have a solid conceptual base for your facts and ideas.

The Writing Process

Before You Start. Perhaps the most important part of the writing process is the thinking you do before actually starting to write. If you have a clear idea about what you want to say and why, it will come across in your writing. This pre-writing stage can be broken down into a series of steps, as follows:

1. Be sure you understand exactly what you are expected to do. Read the instructions carefully, and then read them again. If you are unsure about something, *ask.* For exams, be sure you understand whether you are to answer all the essay questions listed or choose one or two of them. For term papers, be sure you understand what is expected in terms of length, treatment of bibliographic material, and the like.
2. Be sure you know exactly what you are going to write about. If you are choosing a topic, try to choose one that you are interested in and about which you know something. Make sure it is not so broad that you could write a book about it; set limits on the topic. Think about what you really want to write about—the thesis—and then state it in a sentence. In the case of date rape, you could write about how date rape is covered by the media, about trends in the reporting of incidents of date rape, about feminist views on the subject, and so on. Each of these could be the subject of a long paper. If you were to write about the reporting of incidents of date rape, your thesis statement might be, "The number of reported incidents of date rape has been increasing because women are more willing to talk about their experience."
3. Make a rough list of the aspects of the topic about which you will be writing. Just jot them down; do not worry about organizing them. Making lists is especially important when answering essay questions on exams. If you have to list items in the margin of the test paper, go ahead. This step is too important to be skipped.
4. Think about the items on your list. How do they relate to one another? Which ones should be discussed first so that the later ones make more sense? Is there an obvious order in which they should be discussed, such as chronological order? Rearrange the items in a logical order before you start writing.
5. (This step applies to longer assignments.) Make an outline based on your list, and as you think of additional points to be made, work them into the outline. The outline does not have to be a formal document with roman numerals, capital letters, and so on. It just has to make clear which items are the main points and which items are supporting arguments and examples. Do not start writing until you have organized and outlined the material you are going to cover. Outlining may seem like a waste of time, and it is often avoided even by professional writers. But it is an essential skill. With a good outline, a paper or report will practically write itself. On the other hand, when material is not organized beforehand, the writing process is likely to be laborious and time consuming.

The First Draft. In writing your first draft, pay special attention to the introduction. It is the most important part of your essay or paper; it sets forth your argument and gets the reader's attention. Throughout the paper, follow your outline even if you are tempted to depart from it. Going off on tangents will take up valuable time and weaken your argument.

At this stage it is important to let your ideas flow even if your sentences sound a bit awkward and you are not sure exactly which words to use. Matters of style and usage can be dealt with when you revise your draft. Keep in mind, however, that no amount of revision will turn a sloppy, poorly thought out paper into a good one. At any stage of the writing process you should avoid pretentious and meaningless phrasing and wordiness. As the noted essayist George Orwell put it, "Words like *phenomenon, element, individual* (as noun), *objective, categorical, effective, virtual, basic, primary, promote, constitute, exhibit, exploit, utilize, eliminate, liquidate,* are used to dress up simple statements and give an air of scientific impartiality to biased judgments." Orwell illustrates his point with the following example, using a well-known verse from *Ecclesiastes:*

> I returned and saw under the sun, that the race is not to the swift, nor the battle to the strong, neither yet bread to the wise, nor yet riches to men of understanding, nor yet favour to men of skill; but time and chance happeneth to them all.

Here is the same verse, rewritten by Orwell in clumsy, pretentious prose:

> Objective consideration of contemporary phenomena compels the conclusion that success or failure in competitive activities exhibits no tendency to be commensurate with innate capacity, but that a considerable element of the unpredictable must invariably be taken into account.

(1949, p. 360)

Revising. Peg Bracken, author of the *I Hate to Cook Book,* has this to say about leftovers: "When in doubt, throw it out." The same could be said about revising. Do not become wedded to your words—sometimes your most useful tool is the wastebasket.

It is important to be tough on yourself when you revise. If a sentence does not say what you want it to say, rewrite it or write a new one. If a word is not quite right, use another one. If your paragraphs are too long, shorten them. Rarely will the original version be better than the revised one.

Revision is an essential part of the writing process. Do not skip it—bite the bullet and *do* it! (Actually, do it two or three times.) Revise your introductory paragraphs last—they are the most important part of the paper because they are intended to get the reader's attention. Try putting yourself in the reader's shoes and read your opening paragraphs. Do they state the subject clearly? Will they grab the reader's attention? If not, rewrite them.

The process of writing, revising, and preparing the final version is much easier if it is done on a computer using a word-processing program. Some tips for writing with a word processor are presented on pages 36 and 37.

Preparing the Final Version. When you are satisfied with what you have written, you are ready to prepare the final version of the paper. Before you do so, check your spelling and punctuation. You can use a spell-checker program, but you must proofread the material yourself as well; the spell checker will not catch certain kinds of errors. It is a good idea to add a table of contents listing the main sections of the paper, and be sure to include a bibliography in the style required by your instructor.

The final version of the paper should be double spaced, with one-inch margins, on 8-1/2" × 11" plain bond paper.

Improving Your Writing Style

If you feel confident that you have said what you want to say but believe that you could say it better, you are concerned about your writing style. It is not difficult to improve your style if you consider some of the suggestions and guidelines provided by experts in the field. Among the best-known books on this subject is *The Elements of Style,* by William Strunk and E. B. White. We strongly recommend that you purchase a copy of this refreshingly short book; it is almost certainly available in your college bookstore.

Strunk and White provide the following guidelines for developing a good writing style:

1. Put yourself in the background.
2. Write in a way that comes naturally.
3. Write with nouns and verbs.
4. Do not overstate.
5. Avoid the use of qualifiers (*very, somewhat,* and so on).
6. Do not affect a breezy manner.

7. Use orthodox spelling. (Avoid spellings such as *nite* and *thru*.)
8. Do not explain too much.
9. Do not construct awkward adverbs (*tangledly, tiredly,* and so on).
10. Make sure the reader knows who is speaking.
11. Do not inject opinion.
12. Use figures of speech sparingly.
13. Do not take shortcuts at the cost of clarity.
14. Avoid foreign languages. (Readers will not be impressed by phrases such as "a certain *je ne sais quoi*.")
15. Prefer the standard to the offbeat.

George Orwell has written eloquently on this subject as well. He has this to say about style:

> When you think of a concrete object, you think wordlessly, and then, if you want to describe the thing you have been visualizing you probably hunt about till you find the exact words that seem to fit it. When you think of something abstract you are more inclined to use words from the start, and unless you make a conscious effort to prevent it, the existing dialect will come rushing in and do the job for you, at the expense of blurring or even changing your meaning. Probably it is better to put off using words as long as possible and get one's meaning as clear as one can through pictures or sensations. Afterward one can choose—not simply *accept*—the phrases that will best cover the meaning, and then switch round and decide what impression one's words are likely to make on another person. This last effort of the mind cuts out all stale or mixed images, all prefabricated phrases, needless repetitions, and humbug and vagueness generally. But one can often be in doubt about the effect of a word or a phrase, and one needs rules that one can rely on when instinct fails. I think the following rules will cover most cases:
>
> (i) Never use a metaphor, simile, or other figure of speech which you are used to seeing in print.
> (ii) Never use a long word where a short one will do.
> (iii) If it is possible to cut a word out, always cut it out.
> (iv) Never use the passive where you can use the active.
> (v) Never use a foreign phrase, a scientific word, or a jargon word if you can think of an everyday English equivalent.
> (vi) Break any of these rules sooner than say anything outright barbarous.

(1949, pp. 365–366)

Avoiding Sexist Language

It is essential to avoid sexist language in your writing, but you also want to avoid twisting the language or writing in an unnatural fashion. A few basic rules can help you avoid both extremes:

1. Keep in mind that occupation or profession is independent of sex. Do not imply that all home-makers or secretaries are women or that all managers or professors are men.
2. When using a pronoun to refer to an antecedent who could be of either sex, such as "the teacher," use *he or she, him or her, his or her*. Or use the plural—"teachers . . . they . . . "
3. Avoid nouns ending in -*man* unless they apply to an identified male. Words such as *head* or *chair* can be used instead of *chairman, police officer* instead of *policeman, letter carrier* instead of *mailman*.
4. Use *humanity* rather than *mankind* in referring to the human race.

Avoiding Common Mistakes

Certain errors of spelling and usage crop up in many people's writing. Some words are frequently misused because they are confused with words they resemble. Others are considered unsuitable in formal writing; they include informal words and phrases (colloquialisms) and slang. There are also certain expressions that are considered nonstandard and should be avoided. The following list presents some of the most frequently misused words and expressions.

a, an.   Use *a* before a word beginning with a consonant sound: *a* car, *a* hat, *a* history test, *a* union (*u* pronounced as if preceded by consonant *y*).

Use *an* before a word beginning with a vowel sound: *an* accident, *an* image, *an* honest person, (*h* is silent), *an* uncle.

accept, except.   *Accept* (verb) means "to receive": She *accepted* the gift.

Except (usually preposition) means "excluding": Everyone clapped *except* Farley.

Note: *Except* is occasionally a verb, meaning "to exclude": If you *except* the fifth clause, the rule applies in her case.

actual fact.   See *fact*.

adapt, adopt.   *Adapt* means "to adjust or make suitable." It is usually followed by *to*: He *adapted to* his new social environment.

Adopt means "to take as one's own": He *adopted* the habits of his new social environment. They *adopted* a child.

advice, advise.   *Advice* (noun) means "counsel": Take my *advice*.
Advise (verb) means "to give advice": I *advise* you to go.

affect, effect.   Most commonly, *affect* (verb) means "to influence": The war *affected* everyone.

Most commonly, *effect* (noun) means "a result": One *effect* of the war was mass starvation.

Note: Less commonly, *affect* (as a verb) means "to pretend or imitate": He *affected* a British accent. *Effect* (as a verb) means "to accomplish, to bring about": The medicine *effected* a cure.

aggravate.   Colloquial when used for *irritate* or *annoy*: The children *annoyed* (not *aggravated*) him.

aisle, isle.   An *aisle* is a passage between rows of seats. An *isle* is an island.

all, all of.   *All of* is redundant when used with common nouns: *All* (not *all of*) the men arrived on time.

allusion, illusion, delusion.   *Allusion* means "an indirect reference": Her Biblical *allusions* drew praise.

Illusion means "a false perception eventually recognized as false": It was an optical *illusion*.

Delusion refers to a false perception or belief that is held as a result of self-deception: He labored under the *delusion* that everyone admired him.

almost.   See *most*.

a lot, alot, allot.   *A lot* is colloquial when used for *many* or *much*: He had *many* (not *a lot of*) relatives. He was *much* (not *a lot*) better. Avoid the misspelling *alot*.

Allot means "to apportion or give by some plan": The officials will *allot* each large family a subsidy.

already, all ready.   Use *all ready* (meaning "completely ready") wherever *ready* alone makes sense: The squad was *all ready*. (The squad was *ready*.)

Elsewhere, use *already* (meaning "previously" or "by this time"): She had *already* eaten. He is here *already*.

alright.   Incorrect for *all right*.

altogether, all together.   Use *all together* (meaning "in a group") wherever *together* alone makes sense: We were *all together* at the party. (We were *together* at the party.)

Elsewhere use *altogether* (meaning "wholly, completely, in all"): Custer was *altogether* surprised at Little Big Horn.

alumna, alumnus.   An *alumna* is a female former student of a school or college. The plural is *alumnae* (usually pronounced with a final sound of *EE*).

An *alumnus* is the male or mixed-gender equivalent; the plural is *alumni* (usually pronounced with the final sound of *EYE*).

always. Do not contradict *always* (meaning "all the time") by adding *generally* or *usually* (meaning "most of the time") as a modifier.

Wrong: She *generally* (or *usually*) *always* wins.

Right: She *always* (or *usually* or *generally*) wins.

among. See *between.*

amoral, immoral. *Amoral* means "not concerned with morality": An infant's acts are *amoral.* *Immoral* means "against morality": Murder is *immoral.*

amount, number. *Amount* refers to things in bulk or mass: a large *amount* of grain; no *amount* of persuasion.

Number refers to countable objects: a *number* of apples.

and etc. See *etc.*

and/or. Avoid it except in legal and business writing:

Weak: Linda plans to get a degree in psychology *and/or* education.

Better: Linda plans to get a degree in psychology, education, or both.

angry at, about, with. One becomes *angry at* or *about* a thing but *angry with* a person. See also *mad.*

ante-, anti-. Both are prefixes. *Ante-* means "before": *anteroom, antedate.*

Anti- means "against": *antibody, antisocial.*

anxious, eager. *Anxious* conveys worry or unease: She is *anxious* about her safety.

Eager conveys strong desire: He is *eager* to eat.

anymore, any more. *Any more* means "additional": Are there *any more* noodles?

Anymore means "at present": You don't call *anymore.*

anyone, any one. *Anyone* means "any person": Has *anyone* here seen Kelly?

Any one refers to any single item of a number of items: If you like my drawings, take *any one* you wish.

anyone, everyone, someone, anybody, everybody, somebody. Use a singular verb and pronoun with these words.

anyplace, everyplace, noplace, someplace. Colloquial. Precise writers and speakers prefer *anywhere, everywhere, nowhere, somewhere.*

anyways. Nonstandard; use *anyway* or *any way.*

anywheres, everywheres, nowheres, somewheres. Nonstandard; use *anywhere, everywhere,* and so on.

apt, likely, liable. *Apt* is used when probability is based on normal, habitual, or customary tendency: She is *apt* to blush when embarrassed.

Likely indicates mere probability: It is *likely* to rain tomorrow.

Liable indicates an undesirable or undesired risk: He's *liable* to harm himself by playing with a loaded gun.

aren't I. Obviously ungrammatical (*are I not*), though some authorities accept it in informal use. *Am I not* is the alternative.

as, because, since. To express cause, make *because* your first choice; it is most precise.

As and *since* may be ambiguous, conveying either a time or cause relation: *Since* you left, I've been sick.

Since is acceptable informally when there is no ambiguity. *As* is the least acceptable.

as, like. See *like.*

at. Redundant with *where*: *Where* is she? (not *Where* is she *at*?)

aural.   See verbal.

awful, awfully.   *Awful* is colloquial when used adverbially to mean "very bad, ugly, shocking": His language was *shocking* (not *awful*).

Awful is incorrect when used adverbially to mean "very": That pizza was *very* (not *awful*) good.

Awfully is colloquial when used to mean "very": Jan is *very* (not *awfully*) happy.

awhile.   Do not use the adverb *awhile* after *for*. One may stay *awhile* (adverb), stay a *while* (noun), stay for a *while* (noun), but not for *awhile* (adverb).

bad, badly.   *Badly* (adverb) is colloquial when used for *very much* or *greatly* or after a linking verb (*be, seem,* and so on): She wanted *very much* (not *badly*) to be there.

Bad (adjective) correctly follows a linking verb: I feel *bad.*

because.   See *reason is because* and *as, because, since.*

being as (how), being that.   Colloquial or nonstandard for *as, because,* or *since* (which see).

beside, besides.   *Beside* (preposition) means "by the side of": A man was sitting *beside* me (in the seat next to mine).

Besides (preposition) means "in addition to" or "except": Only one man was sitting *besides* me (everyone else was standing). As a conjunctive adverb, it means "in addition": He is ugly; *besides,* he is boorish.

better, had better.   Always add *had* or its contraction, *'d,* before *better* when you mean *should* or *ought to*:

Wrong: You *better* milk the cows.

Right: You *had* (or You*'d*) better milk the cows.

between.   A preposition; the objective case must follow it: *between* you and *me,* not *between* you and *I.*

between, among.   *Between* implies *two* persons or things in a relationship; *among* implies *three or more*; Must I decide *between* cake and ice cream? The estate was divided *among* the five children.

born, borne.   For all meanings of *bear* except "give birth," the past participle is *borne. Borne* is correct in this sense also when it follows *have* or precedes *by*: Mrs. Jackson had already *borne* six children. The half-sisters were *borne* by different mothers.

Born is the correct past participle in other contexts relating to birth: The child was *born* in Brazil.

brake, break.   *Brake* refers to stopping: Apply the *brake. Brake* the car carefully.

Break refers to destroying, damaging, exceeding, or interrupting: Don't *break* the glass. I'll *break* the record. Take a ten-minute *break.*

bring, take.   Precise usage requires *bring* when you mean "to come (here) with" and *take* when you mean "to go (there) with."

bunch.   Colloquial when meaning "crowd; group of people." Say "a *bunch* of bananas" but not "a *bunch* of friends."

bust, busted, bursted.   Incorrect forms of the verb *burst,* of which the three principal parts are *burst, burst, burst*: Yesterday the water pipes *burst* (or *had burst*).

but that, but what.   Colloquial for *that*: I don't doubt *that* (not *but that*) he'll come.

but yet.   Redundant; use either: old *but* good; old *yet* good.

can, may.   *Can* means "to be able": *Can* he lift the log? *May* means "to have permission": *May* I go with you?

can't hardly, can't scarcely.   A double negative. Say "I *can't* hear her" or "I *can hardly* (or *can scarcely*) hear her."

can't help but.   Colloquial for *can't help*:

Colloquial: I *can't help but* admire him.

Formal: I *can't help* admiring him.

canvas, canvass.   A *canvas* is a cloth: Buy a *canvas* tent.

Canvass means "to solicit": *Canvass* the area for votes.

capital, capitol.   Use *capitol* for the building where a legislature meets: The senator posed on the steps of the state *capitol*.

Elsewhere, use *capital*: Albany is the state *capital* (chief city). The firm has little *capital* (money). It was a *capital* (first rate) idea. The defendant has committed a *capital* offense (one punishable by death).

carat, caret, carrot.   Gold and gems are weighed in *carats*. A *caret* (∧) signals an omission: I ∧ going home. A *carrot* is a vegetable: Eat your *carrots*.

casual, causal.   *Casual* means "occurring by chance, informal, unplanned"; *causal* means "involving cause."

censor, censure.   To *censor* is to examine written, filmed, or broadcast material to delete objectionable content: How dare you *censor* my article!

To *censure* is to criticize or blame: The officer was *censured* for misconduct.

cite, site, sight.   *Cite* means "quote an authority or give an example": He will *cite* Shakespeare's sonnet about age.

Site means "location": Here is the new building *site*.

Sight refers to seeing: His *sight* was failing. They have *sighted* the enemy.

classic, classical.   *Classic* means "of the highest class or quality": *War and Peace* is a *classic* novel.

Classical means "pertaining to the art and life of ancient Greece and Rome": Mae is in Greece studying *classical* art. *Classical* music refers to symphonies, opera, and the like.

coarse, course.   *Coarse* means "rough, not fine": *coarse* wool.

A *course* is a path or a series of lessons: race *course*, art *course*.

compare to, compare with.   *Compare to* means "to point out one or more similarities": Sports writers are *comparing* the rookie *to* Hank Aaron.

Compare with means "to examine in order to find similarities and differences": Have you ever *compared* the new Ford *with* the Plymouth?

compliment, complement.   *Compliment* means "to express praise": He *complimented* Beatrice on her good taste.

Complement means "to complete, enhance, or bring to perfection": The illustrations should *complement* the text.

The nouns *compliment* and *complement* are distinguished similarly.

comprise, compose, include.   *Comprise* means "to be made up of (in entirety)": New York City *comprises* five boroughs.

Compose means the opposite, "to make up": Five boroughs *compose* New York City.

Include means "to contain (but not necessarily in entirety)": New York City *includes* the boroughs of Brooklyn and Queens.

connect up.   See *up*.

consensus.   Avoid the trite and redundant *consensus of opinion*. Use *consensus* alone ("general agreement").

contact.   *Contact* as a verb meaning "to get in touch with" is still not acceptable in formal writing. *Contact* as a noun meaning "source" has become accepted.

continual, continuous.   *Continual* means "frequently repeated": He worked in spite of continual interruptions.

Continuous means "without interruption": We heard the *continuous* roar of the falls.

continued on.   Often redundant; omit *on*: We *continued* (not *continued on*) our journey. But: We *continued on* Highway 280.

convince, persuade.   *Convince* emphasizes changing a person's belief: *Convince* me of your sincerity.

Persuade emphasizes moving a person to action: The officer's speech *persuaded* Pat to enlist.

correspond to, correspond with.   *Correspond to* means "to be similar or analogous to": Our Congress *corresponds to* the British Parliament.

Correspond with also means "to communicate with through exchange of letters."

could of, might of, ought to of, should of, would of.   All wrong; *of* results from mishearing the contraction *'ve* (*have*). Write *could have, would have,* and so on.

council, counsel, consul.   *Council* means "a deliberative assembly of persons": The city *council* convenes at noon.

Counsel (noun) means "advice" or "attorney": He gave me good *counsel* when he told me to stop procrastinating. The *counsel* for the defense filed an appeal.

Counsel (verb) means "to give advice": He will *counsel* me about postgraduate plans.

Consul means "an officer in the foreign service": The distinguished guest was the *consul* from Spain.

credible, credulous, creditable.   *Credible* means "believable": A good witness should be *credible*.

Credulous means "too ready to believe; gullible": A *credulous* person is easily duped.

Creditable means "praiseworthy": The young pianist gave a *creditable* performance of a difficult work.

data, phenomena, strata, media.   These are plural forms: Those *data* are available. The singular forms are *datum* (rarely used), *phenomenon, stratum, medium.*

Note: *Data* is gaining acceptance also as a singular when it refers to a single mass of information: All your *data* has been lost.

decent, descent.   *Decent* means "proper, right": It's the *decent* thing to do.
Descent means "a going down" or "ancestry": The *descent* was steep. She's of Welsh *descent.*

delusion.   See *allusion.*

device, devise.   A *device* (noun) is an invention or a piece of equipment: I made this *device.*
To *devise* (verb) is to invent: *Devise* a new mousetrap.

different from, different than.   Formal usage requires *different from*: Her dress is *different from* yours. The tendency is growing, however, to accept *different than* when a clause follows, since it seems simpler: His response was *different than* (rather than *different from what*) I expected.

differ from, differ with.   *Differ from* expresses unlikeness: This book *differs from* the others in giving more details.

Differ with expresses divergence of opinion: I *differ with* you about the importance of the tax bill.

discuss, discus, disgust.   To *discuss* is to talk: Let's *discuss* the election.
A *discus* is a disc-shaped object: Throw the *discus.*
Disgust refers to being offensive: War *disgusts* me.

disinterested, uninterested.   *Uninterested* means simply "not interested": Pat is *uninterested* in mechanics.

Disinterested means "not influenced by personal interest; impartial, unbiased": Only a truly *disinterested* person should serve as an arbitrator.

dived, dove.   *Dived* is the preferred past tense and past participle of *dive*: The youngsters *dived* (not *dove*) for coins.

due (to).   *Due to* is in common use as a preposition. However, strict usage requires *because of*: We were late *because of* (not *due to*) traffic.
Due to is correct as an adjective following a linking verb: Our lateness was *due to* traffic.
See also *fact that*.

each and every.   Redundant; use either: "*each* of us," "*every* one of us," but not "*each and every* one of us."

each other, one another.   *Each other* refers to *two* persons or things, *one another* refers to *three or more*.

eager.   See *anxious*.

effect.   See *affect*.

elicit, illicit.   To *elicit* is to draw forth: *Elicit* some response. *Illicit* means "illegal": Shun *illicit* drugs.

emigrate, immigrate.   *Emigrate* means "to leave a country"; *immigrate* means "to enter a new country": Millions *emigrated* from Europe. They *immigrated* to America.

eminent, imminent.   *Eminent* means "distinguished": She's an *eminent* surgeon.
Imminent means "about to happen": Rain is *imminent*.

end up.   See *up*.

ensure, insure.   Use *insure* when referring to insurance (protection against loss): You should *insure* your house.
Ensure is often preferred for "make sure, make safe": These tires will *ensure* that you'll never skid.

enthuse.   Colloquial for *become enthusiastic*: She *becomes enthusiastic* (not *enthuses*) about everything.

envelop, envelope.   To *envelop* is to surround: Fog *envelops* us.
An *envelope* holds a letter: Seal the *envelope*.

etc.   Avoid *etc.* (meaning "and others") in formal paragraph writing. Use *and others* or *and so forth*. Better, rephrase the sentence to avoid all of these:
Weak: Jill prefers reading Twain, Howells, *and so forth*.
Better: Jill prefers writers *such as* Twain and Howells.
Always avoid *and etc.*; it is redundant.

everybody.   See *anyone*.

everyone, every one.   Use *everyone* where you can substitute *everybody*: *Everyone* (*everybody*) wishes you well. Elsewhere, use *every one* (usually followed by *of*): *Every one* of the roses died. See also *anyone*.

everyplace, everywheres.   See *anyplace, anywheres*.

every so often.   Colloquial for *occasionally*. Also colloquial: *every which way, every bit as, every once in a while*.

except.   See *accept*.

fact.   *Actual fact, real fact,* and *true fact* are usually redundant.

fact that.   Wordy. For *due to the fact that*, say *because*; for *except for the fact that*, say *except that*; or recast the sentence:
Wordy: *Due to the fact that he was late*, we lost.
Concise: We lost *because he was late*.

Wordy: *The fact that he was late* made us lose.

Concise: *His lateness* made us lose.

famous, notable, notorious.   *Famous* means "widely known"; it usually has favorable connotations.

Notable means "worthy of note" or "prominent"; a person can be *notable* without being *famous*.

Notorious means "widely known in an unfavorable way": Bluebeard was *notorious* for being a bad husband.

farther, further.   *Farther* refers to distance: He walked *farther* than I did.
Further means "to a greater extent or degree": Let's discuss the matter *further*.

fewer, less. Use *fewer* with countable things; *fewer* refers to number: She has *fewer* assets than I have.

Use *less* with things that are not countable but are considered in bulk or mass; *less* refers to quantity: She has *less* wealth than I have.

fine.   The adjective *fine* is much overused as a vague word of approval, as "a *fine* boy." Use a more precise word. As an adverb meaning "well" ("He does *fine*"), it is colloquial. *Fine* also means "subtle" or "not coarse."

folks.   Colloquial for *family, relatives, people*.

formally, formerly. *Formally* means "according to proper form": Introduce us *formally*.
Formerly means "previously": They *formerly* lived here.

former, first; latter, last.   *Former* and *latter* refer to the first and second named of two; *first* and *last* refer to items in a series.

forth, fourth.   *Forth* means "forward": Go *forth* and conquer.
Fourth is 4th: I was *fourth* in line.

funny.   Do not use in formal writing to mean "odd" or "peculiar."

generally always.   See *always*.

good.   Do not use this adjective for the adverb *well*: The car runs *well* (not *good*).

As an adjective, *good* may correctly follow a linking verb: She feels *good* about winning.

got.   See *have got*.

had of.   Incorrect for *had*: I wish I *had* (or *I'd*—not *I had of* or *I'd of*) seen the show.

had ought.   Incorrect for *ought*: I *ought* (not *had ought*) to go.
Hadn't ought is also incorrect. Use *ought not*.

half.   Say *a half* or *half a(n)*, not *a half a(n)*: Fill a *half* page (or *half a* page, but not *a half a* page).

hanged, hung.   *Hanged* means "executed": Judas *hanged* himself.
Hung means "suspended": The picture was *hung*.

hardly.   See *can't hardly*.

have got.   Colloquial for *have*: I *have* (not *have got*) a dollar.

healthy, healthful.   *Healthy* means "possessing health": The children are *healthy*.
Healthful means "conducive to health": Good food is *healthful*.

help.   See *can't help but*.

herself, himself, myself, yourself.   Do not substitute these intensive pronouns for the personal pronouns *I, you, him, her*: Grace and *you* (not *yourself*) are invited. She sent tickets to Don and *me* (not *myself*).

hisself.   Incorrect for *himself*. He blames *himself* (not *hisself*) for the accident.

historic, historical.   Strictly, *historic* means "famous or important in history": July 4, 1776, is a *historic* date.

    Historical means "pertaining to history": Verna reads *historical* novels.

hopefully.   Strictly, it means "full of hope": Christy *hopefully* awaited the posting of grades. In formal use, avoid it in the sense of "it is hoped that": *We hope that* (not *Hopefully*) the train will arrive on time.

how.   See *being as (how), seeing as how.*

if, whether.   *If* can be unclear when used to introduce alternative conditions. "Tell us *if* you see him" can mean not only "Tell us *whether (or not)* you see him" but also "*In case* you ever see him, tell us." Use *whether* for clarity.

illicit.   See *elicit.*

illusion.   See *allusion.*

immigrate.   See *emigrate.*

imminent.   See *eminent.*

immoral.   See *amoral.*

imply, infer.   The writer or speaker *implies*; the reader or listener *infers*.

    Imply means "to state indirectly or suggest": He *implied* that we were at fault.

    Infer means "to draw a conclusion or derive by reasoning": I *inferred* from his statement that he blamed us.

in, into.   *Into* indicates movement from outside to inside: Fido ran *into* the house.

    Otherwise, use *in*: Fido stays *in* the house at night.

in back of.   Colloquial for *behind, at the back of, back of.*

include.   See *comprise.*

incredible, incredulous.   A fact or happening is *incredible* (unbelievable): Her thirty-foot putt was *incredible*.

    A person is *incredulous* (unbelieving): He was *incredulous* when told of her thirty-foot putt.

individual, person, party.   Do not use *party* or *individual* when you mean simply *person*: A person (not an *individual* or a *party*) that I met told me the news.

    Except in legal and telephone-company language, and when you mean "one taking part," do not use *party* to refer to one person.

    Use *individual* only when emphasizing a person's singleness: Will you act with the group or as an *individual*?

ingenious, ingenuous.   *Ingenious* means "clever"; *ingenuous* means "naive, frank."

in regards to.   Incorrect for *in regard to*, or *as regards.*

inside of.   Often redundant; omit *of* or use *within*: He was *inside* (not *inside of*) the room.

    Inside of is colloquial when used in reference to time or distance: I shall come *within* (not *inside of*) an hour. I was *within* (not *inside of*) a mile of my destination.

    "The *inside* of the house" is correct; here, *inside* is a noun.

instance, instant, instant's.   *Instance* means "a case or example": He cited an *instance* of discrimination.

    Instant (noun) means "a brief time, a particular point in time, a moment": Come here this *instant*!

    Instant (adjective) means "urgent or immediate": An *instant* need is food for the poor. Do you like *instant* coffee?

    Instant's is the possessive form of the noun *instant*: He came at an *instant's* notice.

insure.　See *ensure.*

irregardless.　There is no such word. Use *regardless.*

irrelevant.　This word means "not related to the point or subject." Notice the letters *rel* as in *related.* There is no such word as *irrevelant.*

isle.　See *aisle.*

is when, is where.　Avoid both expressions except when referring to a time or place:

　　Wrong:　A treaty *is when* nations sign an agreement.

　　Right:　A treaty *is* a signed agreement among nations.

　　Right:　Home *is where* the heart is. (place)

it being.　An awkward substitute for *since it is.*

its, it's.　*Its* is the possessive of *it*: The dog wagged *its* tail.

　　It's is the contraction of *it is.* Use *it's* only if you can correctly substitute *it is* in your sentence: *It's* (*It is*) the best thing.

kid, kids.　Colloquial for *child, children.*

kind of, sort of.　Colloquial if used for *somewhat* or *rather.*

kind of a, sort of a.　Omit the *a.* He wanted *some kind of* (not *some kind of a*) book.

last, latter.　See *former.*

later, latter.　*Later,* the comparative form of *late,* means "more late."

　　Latter refers to the second of two things mentioned. If more than two are mentioned, use *last* instead of *latter.*

lay.　See *lie.*

lead, led.　*Lead* (rhymes with *need*) is the present tense of the verb meaning "to conduct, to go at the head of, to show the way": She can *lead* us to safety.

　　Led is the past tense and past participle of the same verb: She *led* us to safety. She has *led* us to safety.

　　Lead (rhymes with *dead*) is a metal: I need a *lead* pipe.

learn, teach.　*Learn* means "to acquire knowledge": We *learned* irregular verbs.
　　Teach means "to impart knowledge": The professor *taught* us irregular verbs.

leave, let.　*Leave* means "to depart": I must *leave* now.
　　Let means "to permit": *Let* me go.

less.　See *fewer.*

lessen, lesson.　To *lessen* is to diminish: His pain *lessened.*

　　A *lesson* is a unit of learning: Study your *lesson.*

liable, likely.　See *apt.*

lie, lay.　*Lie* means "to rest" and is an intransitive verb (it never takes an object): He makes me *lie* down in green pastures. The islands *lie* under the tropical sun. Here *lies* Jeremiah Todd.

　　Lay means "to put, to place," and is a transitive verb (it must take an object): *lay* your *head* on this pillow. Let me *lay* your fears to rest.

　　To complicate matters, the past tense of *lie* is spelled and pronounced the same as the present tense of *lay*:

Present	Past	Past Participle
lie (rest)	lay (rested)	(has) lain (rested)
lay (place)	laid (placed)	(has) laid (placed)

Yesterday Sandra *lay* (rested) too long in the sun. She should not have *lain* (rested) there so long. Yesterday the workers *laid* (placed) the foundation. They have *laid* (placed) it well.

like, as. In formal English, do not use *like* (preposition) where *as* or *as if* (conjunction) sounds right: He looks *as if* (not *like*) he's angry. She died just *as* (not *like*) her mother did.

loose, lose. *Loose* (usually adjective—rhymes with *goose*) is the opposite of *tight* or *confined*: A *loose* coupling caused the wreck. The lions are *loose*!

Loose is also sometimes a verb: *Loose* my bonds.

Lose (verb—rhymes with *news*) is the opposite of *to find* or *win*: Did you *lose* your wallet? We may *lose* the game.

lots, lots of. Colloquial if used for *much* or *many*.

mad, angry. In formal English, do not use *mad* to mean "angry." The common formal meaning of *mad* is "insane" or "insanely foolish": Do not be *angry* with me (not *mad* at me).

marvelous. Overused as a vague word of approval.

may. See *can*.

maybe, may be. *Maybe* is an adverb meaning "perhaps": *Maybe* you should ask her. Do not confuse it with the verb *may be*: He *may be* arriving late tonight.

media. See *data*.

meet up with. See *up*.

might of. See *could of*.

moral, morale. *Moral* (as an adjective) means "righteous, ethical": To pay his debts was a *moral* obligation.

Moral (as a noun) means "a lesson or truth taught in a story": The *moral* of the story is that greed is wrong.

Morale is a noun meaning "spirit": The team's *morale* sagged.

most, almost. Do not use the adjective *most* for the adverb *almost*. *Almost* (not *most*) all my friends came.

myself. See *herself*.

nauseated, nauseous. *Nauseated* means "suffering from nausea": I was *nauseated* from the fumes.

Nauseous means "causing nausea": The *nauseous* fumes overcame me.

nice. Trite and overused as a substitute for *pleasant* or *agreeable* or for indicating approval. Use a specific adjective.

noplace, nowheres. See *anyplace; anywheres*.

notable, notorious. See *famous*.

nowhere near. Colloquial for *not nearly*.

number. See *amount*.

of. See *could of; kind of; kind of a; off of; outside of*.

off of. Usually redundant; omit *of*: Keep *off* (not *off of*) the grass. He jumped *off* (not *off of*) the platform.

O.K., okay. Colloquial for *all right* or *correct*.

one another. See *each other*.

only. Place *only* as close as possible to the word it modifies, to prevent misreading. "I *only lent* her those books" and "I lent her *only those* books" have different meanings.

or.   See *and/or.*

oral.   See *verbal.*

ought to of.   See *could of; had ought.*

outside of.   Colloquial for *besides, except. Of* is redundant when denoting space: She was *outside* (not *outside of*) the store. But "the *outside of* the house" is correct; here *outside* is a noun.

over with.   Redundant; omit *with.*

party, person.   See *individual.*

passed, past.   *Passed* (verb) is from *pass:* I *passed* the test. *Past* (noun) means "a former time": Forget the *past.*

   Past (preposition) means "by, beyond": Walk *past* the gate.

percent (per cent), percentage.   Use *percent* (or *per cent*) with a specific figure: 45 *percent.* Otherwise, use *percentage:* a small *percentage* of voters.

personal, personnel.   *Personal* means "private": It was a *personal* question.
   Personnel are employees: Notify all *personnel.*

persuade.   See *convince.*

phenomena.   See *data.*

plan on.   Do not use in formal English for *plan to:* I *plan to* go (not *plan on going*).

plenty.   Colloquial when used as an adverb: His excuse was *quite* (not *plenty*) good enough for me.
   Plenty is correct as a noun: We have *plenty* of food.

plus.   In general writing, avoid using *plus* for *and:* Jill *and* (not *plus*) all her friends saw you. Jill saw you, *and* (not *plus*) she heard you sing.

practical, practicable.   *Practical* means "useful, sensible, not theoretical"; *practicable* means "feasible, capable of being put into practice": Because they were *practical* women, they submitted a plan that was *practicable.*

precede, proceed.   To *precede* is to come before: X *precedes* Y.
   Proceed means "to go forward": The parade *proceeded.*

presence, presents.   *Presence* means "being present; attendance": Demand their *presence.*
   Presents are gifts, such as birthday *presents.*

pretty.   Colloquial for *large:* The accident will cost him a *large* (not *pretty*) sum.

principle, principal.   A *principle* is a rule or a truth (remember: *principLE* = *ruLE*): The Ten Commandments are moral *principles.* The Pythagorean theorem is a mathematical *principle.*

   Elsewhere, use *principal,* meaning "chief, chief part, chief person": All *principal* roads are closed. At 8 percent, your *principal* will earn $160 interest. The *principal* praised the students.

provided, providing.   Use *provided* (*that*) in preference to *providing* when you mean "on the specific condition that": She will donate twenty dollars *provided that* (not *providing that*) her employer matches it.

quiet, quite.   *Quiet* means "not noisy": This motor is *quiet. Quite* means "very, completely": I'm not *quite* ready.

raise, rise.   *Raise, raised, raised* ("to lift, make come up") is a transitive verb (takes an object): He *raises* vegetables. He *raised* the window.
   Rise, rose, risen ("to ascend") is an intransitive verb (never has an object): The sun is *rising.*

range, vary.   *Range* means "to change or differ within limits": Applicants *ranged* in age from nineteen to thirty years.
   Vary means "to change or differ": Applicants *varied* in age.

real.   Colloquial when used for the adverb *really* or *very*: She was *very* (not *real*) brave.

reason is because.   Redundant. Use *that* instead: The reason he is late is *that* (not *because*) he overslept. Or say *He is late because he overslept.*

regardless, regards.   See *irregardless*; *in regards to.*

respectfully, respectively.   *Respectfully* means "in a manner showing respect": He bowed *respectfully* before the queen. *Respectfully* yours.

   Respectively means "each in the order given": First and second prizes were awarded to Luann and Juan, *respectively.*

Reverend.   Never use *Reverend* alone as a form of address. The title *Reverend* is properly preceded by *the* and is followed by *Mr., Ms., Dr.,* or the first name or initials of the person referred to: We met *the Reverend* Charles Harris (or *the Reverend Mr. Harris*).

right.   Colloquial or archaic when used to mean "directly" or "very": She went *directly* (not *right*) home. He was *very* (not *right*) tired.

right, rite, write.   *Right* means "correct": the *right* answer.

   A *rite* is a ceremony, such as an initiation *rite.*

   To *write* is to put words on paper: *Write* us from Hawaii.

same.   Unless writing a legal document, avoid using *same* for *it* or *them*: We visited Maine and found *it* (not *same*) delightful.

scarcely.   See *can't hardly.*

seeing as how, seeing that.   Incorrect for *since* or *because.*

seldom ever.   Redundant and incorrect for *seldom, hardly ever, seldom if ever, seldom or never.*

shape.   Colloquial if used for *condition*: He was in poor *condition* (not *shape*).

should of.   See *could of.*

sight, site.   See *cite.*

since.   See *as, because, since.*

sit, set.   *Sit, sat, sat* is an intransitive verb (has no object); it means "to be seated": I *sat* on the floor.

   Set, set, set, is a transitive verb (has an object): it means "to put or place": She *set* the *dishes* on the table.

   (*Set* has several intransitive senses, but it is equivalent to *sit* only when one speaks of a hen that *sets* on her eggs.)

so.   *So* is informal when used to introduce a main clause; in formal writing, use *thus* or *therefore,* or recast the sentence:

   Informal: All the crew died, *so* the ship was lost.

   Formal: All the crew died; *thus* the ship was lost.

   Recast: The ship was lost *because* all the crew died.

   Avoid *so* for *very*: I am *very* (not *so*) happy.

   Avoid using *so* for *so that* in clauses of purpose: She came *so that* (not *so*) she might help.

some.   Colloquial if used for *somewhat, a little,* or *quite*: He worried *somewhat* (not *some*). He's *quite* a (not *some*) golfer!

somebody, someone.   See *anyone.*

someplace, somewheres.   See *anyplace; anywheres.*

sort of, sort of a.   See *kind of; kind of a; these kind.*

stationary, stationery.   *Stationary* means "not moving, not movable": This machine is *stationary*. *Stationery* is writing paper.

strata.   See *data*.

such, no such a.   *Such* is colloquial when used for *very*: It is *such* a lovely day. Better: It is a *very* lovely day.

When *such* suggests "what kind" or "how much," it is followed in formal writing by a clause specifying the degree or kind: It was *such* a lovely day *that we went on a picnic*. We saw *such* clouds *that we came home*.

No such a is incorrect for *no such*. There is *no such* (not *no such a*) place.

sure.   Do not use the adjective *sure* for the adverb *surely* or *certainly*: I *surely* (not *sure*) admire her.

Colloquial: "Are you going?" "*Sure*."

sure and.   See *try and*.

take.   See *bring*.

take and, went and.   Redundant: She *hit* (not *took and hit* or *went and hit*) the ball.

teach.   See *learn*.

terribly.   Colloquial when used for *extremely* or *very*: It's *very* (not *terribly*) late.

than, then.   *Than* is a conjunction suggesting difference: He is taller *than* I (am tall). See also *different from*.

Then is an adverb meaning "at that time," "next," or "in that case": *Then* we shall go.

that.   See *being that*; *seeing that*; *this*; *this here*; *who*.

their, there, they're.   *Their* is a possessive pronoun: It is *their* turn.

There is an adverb referring to place: Sit *there*. It is also an expletive (an introductory word): *There* are four of us.

They're is a contraction of *they are*: *They're* on their way.

them.   Do not use for *those*: Watch *those* (not *them*) cars!

these kind, these sort.   *Kind* and *sort* are singular nouns. Do not modify them with the plurals *these* and *those*. Use the singular *this* or *that* instead: I prefer *this* (not these) *kind* of fish. *That* (not *those*) sort of fish will make me sick.

thing.   Avoid this vague noun where you can use a more specific one: Her next *point* (not *The next thing she said*) concerned economic benefits.

this, that, which.   Use only to refer to a definite antecedent.

this here, that there, these here, those there.   Nonstandard for *this, that, these, those*.

those kind, those sort.   See *these kind*.

threw, through.   *Threw* is the past of *throw*: I *threw* the ball. *Through* means "from end to end of." See also next entry.

through, thorough, thought.   *Through* means "from end to end or side to side of": *through* the tunnel.

Thorough means "complete, exact": a *thorough* search.

Thought refers to thinking: a clever *thought*.

thusly.   Incorrect for *thus*.

to, too, two.   *To* is a preposition: She came *to* class. *To* also introduces an infinitive: I wanted *to* hear him.

Too is an adverb meaning "also" or expressing degree: She laughed *too.* He was *too* sick to work. Do not use *too* for *very:* He did not look *very* (not *too*) happy.

Two is a number: I have *two* books.

toward, towards.   Use either, but be consistent.

try and, sure and.   Incorrect for *try to* and *sure to*: Try to (not *try and*) come. Be *sure to* (not *sure and*) call me.

-type.   Avoid needless or illogical use of *-type* as a suffix: She wanted a reflex (not *reflex-type*) camera.

uninterested.   See *disinterested.*

unique.   *Unique* means "having no like or equal." Do not use it with *more, most, very,* or the like: The design was *unique* (not *most unique*).

up.   Often redundant after a verb. Drop *up* unless dropping it changes your meaning: Connect (not *connect up*) the pipes. This road ends (not *ends up*) in a swamp. Climb (not *climb up*) that hill. Gerry and I met (not *met up with*) difficulties.

usage, utilize, use.   *Usage* and *utilize* sound overblown if used where the simple *use* (noun or verb) will do. *Usage* means only "customary use or practice": The book explains English *usage.* *Utilize* means only "to put to some practical or special use": *Utilize* my cane as a splint. Otherwise, stay with *use.*

used to.   The spelling is *used to,* except after *did*: They *used to* date. The flag *used to* have forty-eight stars. *Did*n't he *use to* smoke?

usually always.   See *always.*

vary.   See *range.*

verbal, oral, aural.   *Verbal* means "expressed in words, either written or spoken": An artist's expression may take pictorial, plastic, *verbal,* or other form.

Oral means "uttered or spoken": He gave an *oral* report.

Aural refers to hearing ("of or perceived by the ear").

very.   Do not use this adverb to modify a past participle directly. Use *very* + an adverb such as *much, well*: Her singing was *very much* appreciated (not *very* appreciated).

Avoid overuse of *very. Extremely* and *quite* are good synonyms: She was *quite* (not *very*) embarrassed.

wait on.   *Wait on* means "to attend or serve." It is colloquial if used to mean *wait for*: I waited *for* (not *on*) a bus.

way, ways.   *Way* is colloquial if used for *far*: He lives *far* (not *way*) across the valley.

Way is colloquial in reference to health: She is in *poor health* (not *in a bad way*).

Ways is colloquial for *way* when indicating distance: She lives a little *way* (not *ways*) down the road.

weak, week.   *Weak* means "not strong": *weak* from the flu. A *week* is seven days.

weather, whether.   *Weather* refers to rain, sunshine, and the like.

Whether introduces alternatives: *whether* we live or die.

weird.   Slang when used for *strange, unusual.*

well.   See *good.*

went and.   See *take and.*

what.   See *but what.*

where.   Incorrect when used for *that.* I read in the paper *that* (not *where*) she had arrived.

where . . . at. See *at.*

whether. See *if; weather.*

which. See *this; who.*

while. The strict meaning of *while* is "during the time that." Avoid using it to mean *though* or *whereas*: A century ago many criminals were executed in America, *whereas* (not *while*) today very few are.

who, which, that. Use *who,* not *which,* when referring to people; *which* is only for things. *That* can refer to people or things: The people *who* (or *that,* but not *which*) live here are noisy.

Who may introduce either a restrictive or nonrestrictive clause.

That introduces only restrictive clauses. Many authorities say that *which* should introduce only nonrestrictive clauses, as in "Healy Hall, *which* is on your right, was built in 1878."

who's, whose. *Who's* is a contraction of *who is*: *Who's* that? *Whose* is the possessive of *who*: *Whose* hat is this?

with. See *over with.*

woman, women. *Woman,* like *man,* is singular: that *woman. Women,* like *men,* is plural: those *women.*

wonderful. Trite and overused as an adjective of approval.

worst way. Incorrect for *very much*: I want *very much* to go (not *I want to go in the worst way).*

would have. Use *had,* not *would have,* in an *if* clause:
Wrong: If I *would have* known, I would have left earlier.
Right: If I *had* known, I would have left earlier.

would of. See *could of.*

write. See *right, rite, write.*

yet. See *but yet.*

you all. A southern regionalism for the plural *you.*

your, you're. *Your* is the possessive of *you*: Wear *your* hat. *You're* is a contraction of *you are*: *You're* late.

yourself. See *herself.*

you was. Nonstandard for *you were.*

Source: Blanche Ellsworth, *English Simplified,* 6th ed. (New York: HarperCollins, 1990), pp. 29–36.

Writing with a Word Processor

Most colleges and universities have writing labs equipped with computers, printers, and word-processing software. Today there is almost no excuse for not using these labor-saving tools, especially since a paper produced on a good computer is so much easier to revise and looks so much better in its final form. Even if you do not own your own computer, you should become familiar with a professional-quality word-processing program such as WordPerfect or Microsoft Word. You can learn such a program while working on a paper, and there are almost always people in the writing lab who will be willing to help if you get into a jam. It is a good idea to use the program to write short papers before tackling something more ambitious. Always make sure to back up your files on extra disks so that you do not lose precious research notes and written material as a result of damage or technical problems.

A computer-based word-processing system allows you to revise and polish your writing far more easily than was possible when each new version had to be retyped. Now you can afford to go back over the paper, especially those vital first paragraphs, until each sentence is as finely tuned as you wish. You can easily delete unnecessary words and replace tired clichés with more active words and phrases. You can quickly turn a sentence around so that the most important thought comes first. The computer can offer you no creative help in these matters, but it makes editing your work so easy that instructors are beginning to expect students to hand in more polished writing than they typically did in the past.

Most word-processing programs include spell checkers. But be warned: Spell checkers pick up only words that are misspelled. They do not check for agreement of subject and verb, or for words that are correctly spelled but out of place. If you use *their* when you mean *there*, the spell checker will not reveal the error. So use the spell checker, but remember that it is not a substitute for careful proofreading.

It is always a good idea to print out a rough draft and go over this "hard copy." You cannot see the whole essay or paper on a computer screen the way you can on paper. Also, you cannot as easily decide whether a portion of the paper needs more development or more cutting when you are looking at parts of the paper on a screen.

A final warning: Some students become overly involved in producing attractive papers using a variety of type fonts and other flourishes. This does no harm if you have already produced a first-rate, highly polished paper that meets the terms of the assignment and the standards of good writing. But instructors are highly skeptical of good-looking printouts that seek to mask superficial thinking and lazy editing. So use the word processor to help you be more efficient in your research and writing, not to cover up an inadequate job.

References

Mills, C. W. (1959). *The Sociological Imagination.* New York: Oxford University Press.

Orwell, G. (1949). Politics and the English Language. In *The Orwell Reader.* Fort Worth, TX: Harcourt.

Parsons, T. (1951). *The Social System.* New York: Free Press.

CHAPTER 1

1.1.   In September 1987, villagers in Deorala, India, gathered for the funeral of a young man who had died of a ruptured appendix. During the cremation ceremony the man's distraught widow placed herself on the funeral pyre and died in the flames. It was the first case of *sati* (immolation by a widow) to occur in India in many years; the practice was outlawed in 1829.

Using your sociological imagination, give some reasons why this young widow might have felt compelled to take this drastic step.

_____

_____

_____

_____

_____

_____

_____

_____

_____

_____

_____

_____

_____

_____

_____

_____

_____

_____

_____

_____

1.2.   Refer to Figure 1-1 (p. 10). For each level of analysis, provide two examples of social phenomena that would be analyzed at that level.

Macro	Middle	Micro
_____	_____	_____
_____	_____	_____

1.3.   The chapter points out that people have been thinking about the nature of human societies since the beginning of recorded history. Why, then, did the discipline of sociology not develop until the nineteenth century?

_____

_____

_____

_____

_____

_____

_____

_____

_____

_____

_____

_____

_____

_____

_____

_____

_____

_____

NAME _____   DATE _____

1.4.   There was a time when "gentlemen" who felt that their honor had been challenged would insist on the right to obtain vengeance in a fair fight through a ritual known as a duel. Each duelist brought two other men, known as seconds, to witness the duel. An impartial party started the duel and ensured that it was conducted fairly. Often a duel ended in death, as in the case of Alexander Hamilton, who was killed in a duel with Aaron Burr.

Each of the basic sociological perspectives described in Chapter 1 could be used to explain why duels occurred and why they were eventually outlawed. What aspects of the duel might a functionalist, an interactionist, and a conflict-oriented sociologist emphasize in attempting to explain what is happening?

_____

_____

_____

_____

_____

_____

_____

_____

_____

_____

_____

_____

_____

_____

_____

_____

_____

_____

_____

_____

1.5.   What do sociologists mean when they point to environmental conditions in explaining the biographies of individuals? How does their use of the word *environment* differ from the way environmental lobbyists or "Earth First" activists use the word? When they explain aspects of a person's life in terms of conditions in that individual's environment, do they excuse the individual for his or her own failures or shortcomings?

_____

_____

_____

_____

_____

_____

_____

_____

_____

_____

_____

_____

_____

_____

_____

_____

_____

_____

_____

_____

NAME _____   **DATE** _____

1.6.   Look at the painting entitled *Gleaners* in the photo essay on Art and the Sociological Eye (p. 33). What comments can you make in addition to those in the text accompanying the essay? Do you think the painting implies anything about the types of work that are appropriate for men and women?

_____

_____

_____

_____

_____

_____

_____

_____

_____

_____

_____

_____

_____

_____

_____

_____

_____

_____

_____

_____

CHAPTER 2

2.1. Devise a hypothesis other than those mentioned in the text. What is the dependent variable? the independent variable?

_____

_____

_____

_____

_____

_____

_____

_____

_____

_____

_____

_____

_____

_____

_____

_____

_____

_____

_____

_____

_____

Dependent variable: _____

Independent variable: _____

2.2. Find an example of a questionnaire used in market research or in research by a political candidate or elected official. What kinds of questions are used? Are they worded so as to avoid biasing the answers? Explain.

_____

_____

_____

_____

_____

_____

_____

_____

_____

_____

_____

_____

_____

_____

_____

_____

_____

_____

_____

_____

_____

_____

_____

NAME _____   **DATE** _____

2.3.   (a) Refer to Table 2-2 (p. 53). The table shows that the population of married-couple house-holds declined between 1970 and 1991. By how many percentage points did it decline?

_____

(b) Refer to Table 2-3 (p. 53). This table shows that the proportion of married couples with no chil-

dren _____ between 1970 and 1991.

2.4.   After increasing dramatically during the 1970s, the crime rate in the United States began to decline. At the same time, the number of people in the 15–24 age range also began to decrease. Do you think there is a correlation between these two trends? What information would you seek if you wanted to explore this question further?

_____

_____

_____

_____

_____

_____

_____

_____

_____

_____

_____

_____

_____

_____

_____

_____

_____

2.5.   Abbott Pierce asks an interesting question about possible differences between men's and women's attitudes toward sex (Think about it Critically, p. 60). What steps should he consider before undertaking his own survey on campus? And what problems can you see in the way he words the items on his questionnaire? Give some examples of questions that should be asked in order to study this subject scientifically. Show that the issue is more complicated than Pierce's initial question suggests.

_____

_____

_____

_____

_____

_____

_____

_____

_____

_____

_____

_____

_____

_____

_____

_____

_____

_____

_____

_____

_____

_____

NAME _____   DATE _____

2.6.   Look at the picture of a pornography store in the Visual Sociology section of Chapter 2. Using your sociological imagination, comment on what this photo might imply regarding the uses of pornography and the conflicts it evokes in American society.

_____

_____

_____

_____

_____

_____

_____

_____

_____

_____

_____

_____

_____

_____

_____

_____

_____

_____

_____

_____

_____

_____

_____

CHAPTER 3

3.1. Refer to Figure 3-3 (p. 77) and answer the following questions.

a. How much larger is the world population today that it was in A.D. 1?

_____

b. How large will the world population be by A.D. 2000?

_____

c. When did the world population enter a phase of extremely rapid growth?

_____

3.2. Traditionally, Indian society was made up of a series of castes into which individuals were born and in which they remained for life, regardless of their actions. How would you describe the structure of Indian society?

_____

_____

_____

_____

_____

_____

_____

_____

_____

_____

_____

_____

_____

3.3.   Distinguish between role conflict and role strain, giving examples of each. Why do you think role conflicts are more likely to occur in more complex societies than in simpler ones?

_____

_____

_____

_____

_____

_____

_____

_____

_____

_____

_____

_____

_____

_____

_____

_____

_____

_____

_____

_____

_____

_____

_____

_____

NAME _____ **DATE** _____

3.4. A recent letter to the editor of *The New York Times* suggests that the term *tribe* is useless in describing African peoples. The writer points out that many so-called tribes include numerous language-based ethnic groupings that sometimes conflict with older political groupings. Discuss these comments in light of what you have learned about social structure and social change in the post-colonial world.

_____

_____

_____

_____

_____

_____

_____

_____

_____

_____

_____

_____

_____

_____

_____

_____

_____

_____

_____

3.5.   Why might it be pleasant to live much of one's life in a small town? What drawbacks might there be to living in such a setting? What pleasures and difficulties might one encounter when living in a large city? Do you think it is possible to find gemeinschaft conditions within a large city? If so, give an example of such a situation.

_____

_____

_____

_____

_____

_____

_____

_____

_____

_____

_____

_____

_____

_____

_____

_____

_____

_____

_____

_____

_____

_____

_____

NAME _____   DATE _____

3.6.   Look at the Visual Sociology section of Chapter 3. In what ways does the inauguration of the President of the United States reflect the social structures of American society? What other social structures not seen in these photos are often represented in a presidential inauguration?

_____

_____

_____

_____

_____

_____

_____

_____

_____

_____

_____

_____

_____

_____

_____

_____

_____

_____

_____

_____

_____

_____

_____

CHAPTER 4

4.1. Sixteenth-century Spanish conquistadors characterized many natives of the New World as cannibals. In fact, according to Spanish law, the designation of a tribe as cannibals made it permissible for the conquistadors to enslave its members as they saw fit. What concepts in the sociological study of culture does this highlight?

_____

_____

_____

_____

_____

_____

_____

_____

_____

_____

_____

_____

_____

_____

_____

_____

_____

_____

_____

_____

44   **CHAPTER 4**

4.2.   Refer to the chart in Box 4-1 (p. 110) and provide an example of each of the following:

a. folkways

_____

b. mores

_____

c. misdemeanor laws

_____

d. felonies

_____

4.3.   It has often been pointed out that the Eskimos have numerous words for snow. Does this fact support the linguistic-relativity hypothesis? Why or why not?

_____

_____

_____

_____

_____

_____

_____

_____

_____

_____

_____

_____

_____

_____

_____

_____

_____

NAME _____   **DATE** _____

4.4.   "It's a humiliating time to be a camel in Saudi Arabia," writes Youssef M. Ibrahim in *The New York Times* (April 10, 1989, p. A1). "Gone are the days when Saudi warriors rode their camels into battle at dawn. A fast-food store on Olaya Street is advertising 'Camel Burgers.' Supermarkets sell packaged camel meat, and three professors of animal nutrition at King Saud University are trying to market camel ice cream." Explain these changes in terms of the sociological processes discussed in the chapter.

_____

_____

_____

_____

_____

_____

_____

_____

_____

_____

_____

_____

_____

_____

_____

_____

_____

_____

_____

_____

4.5.   Give three examples of changing social norms. Describe the conflicts surrounding those norms, especially with reference to who is involved in the different sides of the conflict. Briefly describe how such conflicts can be indicators of particular social changes occurring today.

NAME _____   **DATE** _____

4.6. The photo essay that accompanies this chapter depicts Native Americans who have been relocated to large cities. Taken as a group, what do these pictures indicate about the situation of the relocatees?

_____

_____

_____

_____

_____

_____

_____

_____

_____

_____

_____

_____

_____

_____

_____

_____

_____

_____

_____

_____

_____

_____

_____

CHAPTER 5

5.1. The "nature–nurture" controversy has a long history and remains unresolved today. What arguments can be made on both sides of this issue? What is your opinion concerning the relative influence of biological and social factors in creating the person?

_____

_____

_____

_____

_____

_____

_____

_____

_____

_____

_____

_____

_____

_____

_____

_____

_____

_____

5.2. Refer to Box 5-3 (p. 159), then consider the following series of scores: 1, 2, 4, 7, 3, 2, 1, 2, 3, 17, 19.

a. What is the mean? _____

b. What is the median? _____

c. What is the mode? _____

5.3. The case of Genie, the isolated child, raises the age-old speculation that children who have had only minimal contact with other humans offer special research opportunities. What does Genie's case tell scientists about the consequences of a severe lack of childhood socialization? Do researchers still believe that children can be reared by wild animals? In what ways might close observation of how deaf children learn to communicate be a better area of study than further research on children such as Genie?

_____

_____

_____

_____

_____

_____

_____

_____

_____

_____

_____

_____

_____

_____

_____

_____

_____

_____

_____

NAME _____   DATE _____

5.4. In *The Other America*, Michael Harrington wrote: "Once in a slum school in St. Louis, a teacher stopped a fight between two little girls. 'Nice girls don't fight,' she told them. 'Yeah,' one of them replied, 'you should have seen my old lady at the tavern last night.'" Relate this incident to what you have learned about socialization processes and agencies of socialization.

_____

_____

_____

_____

_____

_____

_____

_____

_____

_____

_____

_____

_____

_____

_____

_____

_____

_____

_____

_____

_____

_____

_____

5.5. Recall John B. Watson's claim that if he could only begin early enough in a person's life, he could shape that person into any kind of individual he chose. In theory, this claim might be correct, but in the real world agencies of socialization make it almost impossible for a radical behaviorist such as Watson to control the stimuli experienced by an individual. Explain why this is so.

NAME _____   **DATE** _____

5.6.   Look at the picture of the children with a pigeon in the Visual Sociology section of Chapter 5. What kind of socialization is going on here? What do you think the effects will be on the individual experiencing the socialization?

_____
_____
_____
_____
_____
_____
_____
_____
_____
_____
_____
_____
_____
_____
_____
_____
_____
_____
_____
_____
_____
_____
_____
_____
_____

CHAPTER 6

6.1. Members of the cult known as the Branch Davidians, led by David Koresh, operated as if they were a single primary group even though the group was far larger than most primary groups. What qualities of the group and its leader discouraged the formation of smaller groups (for example, couples or cliques) within the larger group?

_____

_____

_____

_____

_____

_____

_____

_____

_____

_____

_____

_____

_____

_____

_____

_____

_____

_____

_____

_____

6.2. The accompanying table presents the results of an experiment by Daniel Kahneman and his colleagues. Player 1 may divide $10 with Player 2 however he or she wishes, and Player 2 may either accept the amount offered or reject the offer. What do the data imply about the principles guiding the players' decisions?

Total to be divided	$10.00
Average amount offered by Player 1	$4.76
50–50 offers	81%
Average minimum acceptable offer for Player 2	$2.59

_____

_____

_____

_____

_____

_____

_____

_____

_____

_____

_____

_____

_____

_____

_____

_____

_____

_____

_____

_____

NAME _____   **DATE** _____

6.3. "I'm sorry, sir, she's in a meeting. Would you care to leave a message?" Try calling any middle- or upper-level manager; more likely than not, he or she will be in a meeting. But do all these meetings accomplish anything? Recent research on group interaction has found that most of the time groups are not as effective as one person working alone. Can you suggest any reasons why this might be the case and why we continue to share responsibility for decisions in meetings?

_____

_____

_____

_____

_____

_____

_____

_____

_____

_____

_____

_____

_____

_____

_____

_____

_____

_____

_____

_____

_____

_____

6.4. Think of a group in which you participate regularly, such as a committee or work group. Who is the group's task leader? Does someone serve as its socioemotional leader? How did they come to be regarded as leaders by the other members of the group?

_____

_____

_____

_____

_____

_____

_____

_____

_____

_____

_____

_____

_____

_____

_____

_____

_____

_____

_____

_____

_____

NAME _____   DATE _____

6.5.   Review the Critical Response at the end of the chapter summary. It presents a functionalist explanation of the norm of priestly celibacy. Why is this a functionalist explanation?

_____

_____

_____

_____

_____

_____

_____

_____

_____

_____

_____

_____

_____

_____

_____

_____

_____

_____

_____

_____

_____

_____

6.6. The Visual Sociology section of Chapter 6 includes a photo of three young girls running. What kind of group do they represent? Compare this picture with the one of three girls with a doll. What kinds of interaction are likely to occur among the members of both groups?

_____

_____

_____

_____

_____

_____

_____

_____

_____

_____

_____

_____

_____

_____

_____

_____

_____

_____

_____

_____

CHAPTER 7

7.1. In April 1989, in a shocking episode of criminal violence, a rampaging group of teenage boys from a ghetto neighborhood in New York City attacked and raped a young woman who was jogging in Central Park. The episode generated widespread public outcry, and the youths were described as a savage "wolf pack." At about the same time, in the affluent suburb of Glen Ridge, New Jersey, a group of teenage high school athletes were accused of sexually assaulting a slightly retarded female schoolmate. In this case, however, it was said that the young woman may have consented to the encounter and that she had "somewhat of a history of playing with boys provocatively." What are some of the factors that might have contributed to the different reactions to these two crimes?

_____

_____

_____

_____

_____

_____

_____

_____

_____

_____

_____

_____

_____

_____

_____

_____

_____

_____

_____

_____

62   **CHAPTER 7**

7.2.   Refer to Table 7-1 (p. 216) and answer the following questions.

a. In what index category has the rate of crime increased most over the period covered by the table?

_____

b. In what index category is the highest number of crimes committed per 100,000 inhabitants?

_____

c. Is there any index category in which the rate of crime has, on the average, decreased over all or part of the period covered? If so, which one(s)?

_____

7.3.   Watch your daily newspaper for articles about cases that have been settled through plea bargaining. Do you think this is an appropriate way of handling such cases?

_____

_____

_____

_____

_____

_____

_____

_____

_____

_____

_____

_____

_____

_____

_____

_____

_____

_____

_____

NAME _____ **DATE** _____

7.4. A 1992 survey of crime in the five U.S. cities with the largest gay and lesbian communities found that crimes against homosexuals had risen by slightly over 30 percent since the previous year. Gay-rights groups claimed that the public debate about homosexual rights accounted for some of the increase. As a sociologist, explain how the gay-rights movement could lead to more violence against homosexuals. What are your own explanations for the increase in violence directed against homosexuals?

_____

_____

_____

_____

_____

_____

_____

_____

_____

_____

_____

_____

_____

_____

_____

_____

_____

_____

_____

_____

7.5.   Sociologists often claim that if social control depended entirely on the police and the courts, it would be far more dangerous to live in the United States than it is now. Describe what is included in the broader concept of social control underlying this claim.

_____

_____

_____

_____

_____

_____

_____

_____

_____

_____

_____

_____

_____

_____

_____

_____

_____

_____

_____

_____

_____

NAME _____   **DATE** _____

7.6. Look at the photo essay on hoboes at the end of Chapter 7. What do these photos reveal about the life of these socially deviant individuals?

_____

_____

_____

_____

_____

_____

_____

_____

_____

_____

_____

_____

_____

_____

_____

_____

_____

_____

_____

_____

_____

_____

_____

_____

_____

CHAPTER 8

8.1. In the past few years there has been a dramatic increase in the rate of violent crime motivated by racial and ethnic animosities. Researchers studying this phenomenon have found that the majority of the crimes are committed by people in groups of four or more and that the more people in the group, the more vicious the crime. Drawing upon what you have learned in this chapter and others, can you suggest any reasons why this might be the case?

_____

_____

_____

_____

_____

_____

_____

_____

_____

_____

_____

_____

_____

_____

_____

_____

_____

_____

_____

8.2.   During the 1980s, the women's movement, which flourished in the late 1960s and early 1970s, lost momentum. Its leaders no longer agree on the goals of the movement, and many of its members have become disillusioned. On the basis of what you have learned in this chapter, how would you explain this situation?

_____

_____

_____

_____

_____

_____

_____

_____

_____

_____

_____

_____

_____

_____

_____

_____

_____

_____

_____

_____

_____

_____

NAME _____   **DATE** _____

8.3.   Refer to Figure 8–2 (p. 262). By what percentage has the average work week of nonagricultural workers decreased since 1850? Is there evidence that the trend toward a shorter work week will continue?

_____

_____

_____

_____

_____

_____

_____

_____

_____

_____

_____

_____

_____

_____

_____

_____

_____

_____

_____

_____

_____

_____

8.4.   How are public opinion and collective behavior related to each other? Can you give an example of this relationship?

_____

_____

_____

_____

_____

_____

_____

_____

_____

_____

_____

_____

_____

_____

_____

_____

_____

_____

_____

_____

_____

_____

_____

_____

_____

_____

NAME _____   DATE _____

8.5.   What does Malvina Reynolds's song say about the relationship between social movements and civil disobedience? What are some of the risks associated with violent civil disobedience?

_____

_____

_____

_____

_____

_____

_____

_____

_____

_____

_____

_____

_____

_____

_____

_____

_____

_____

_____

_____

_____

_____

8.6. The Visual Sociology feature on MTV shows some young people looking at MTV broadcasts and describing what appeals to them and why. What aspects of the study of social movements and collective behavior do these photos highlight?

_____

_____

_____

_____

_____

_____

_____

_____

_____

_____

_____

_____

_____

_____

_____

_____

_____

_____

_____

_____

_____

_____

_____

NAME _____   DATE _____

CHAPTER 9

9.1. In order to encourage families to have only one child, the Chinese government has instituted a system of incentives and penalties that give enormous advantages to one-child families. Until recently the system met with considerable resistance and was enforced by coercive means. Today, however, more and more couples are complying voluntarily. Why do you think this change is occurring? What long-term consequences might the one-child policy have?

_____

_____

_____

_____

_____

_____

_____

_____

_____

_____

_____

_____

_____

_____

_____

_____

_____

_____

9.2. Refer to Figure 9–1 (p. 297). Are the following statements true or false?

T/F a. Births have exceeded deaths throughout Sweden's history.

T/F b. The period between 1800 and 1850 was a time of rapid growth in the Swedish population.

T/F c. In Sweden the birth and death rates are converging.

9.3. In the wake of the earthquake in San Francisco in 1989, planners attempted to strengthen the unreinforced masonry buildings in the Chinatown section of the city. However, they met with an obstacle: The residents would rather live with the fear of earthquakes than move, even temporarily, as repairs were made. Why do you think this was so?

_____

_____

_____

_____

_____

_____

_____

_____

_____

_____

_____

_____

_____

_____

_____

_____

_____

_____

_____

NAME _____   **DATE** _____

9.4.   What are the major causes of conflict in cities? Describe an instance of such conflict that occurred in the community where you live.

_____

_____

_____

_____

_____

_____

_____

_____

_____

_____

_____

_____

_____

_____

_____

_____

_____

_____

_____

_____

_____

_____

9.5.   What are the dangers of unlimited world population growth? Give some reasons why nations with rapid population growth rates are likely to attempt to curtail the growth of their populations in coming decades. Why might population growth continue at high rates in some of those nations?

_____

_____

_____

_____

_____

_____

_____

_____

_____

_____

_____

_____

_____

_____

_____

_____

_____

_____

_____

_____

_____

_____

NAME _____   **DATE** _____

9.6.   The Visual Sociology section of Chapter 9 shows scenes from the *favelas* of Rio de Janeiro. What do these photos indicate about the process of urbanization? What do they reveal about inequality and conflict in cities?

_____

_____

_____

_____

_____

_____

_____

_____

_____

_____

_____

_____

_____

_____

_____

_____

_____

_____

_____

_____

_____

_____

_____

CHAPTER 10

10.1.   Give examples of social changes that are occurring at the micro, middle, and macro levels of American society today.

_____

_____

_____

_____

_____

_____

_____

_____

_____

_____

_____

_____

_____

_____

_____

_____

_____

_____

_____

_____

_____

_____

10.2.   "Yasmin had a better reason for being nervous than did most Middle Eastern brides," writes Naila Minai in *Women in Islam*. "Although a reputable plastic surgeon had reconstructed her hymen, she wondered if she would pass for a true virgin on her wedding night. With repeated assurances from her mother, who shared her secret, she went off on her honeymoon. A week later she came back with her proudly smiling husband. She had passed the test of virginity."[1] What does this passage reveal about the nature of social change at the micro level?

_____

_____

_____

_____

_____

_____

_____

_____

_____

_____

_____

_____

_____

_____

_____

_____

_____

_____

_____

_____

[1]Naila Minai, *Women in Islam: Tradition and Transition in the Middle East* (New York: Seaview Books, 1981), p. 142.

NAME _____ **DATE** _____

10.3. According to the World Bank's Consultative Group on International Agricultural Research, "Productive agriculture is both an economic and a humanitarian imperative in the developing world . . . In many developing countries, the rural sector is commonly not only the largest but also the most depressed part of society. It provides too little employment and too little production to raise living standards and prepare the way for further advance." Comment on this statement in light of what you have learned about the processes of modernization.

_____

_____

_____

_____

_____

_____

_____

_____

_____

_____

_____

_____

_____

_____

_____

_____

_____

_____

_____

_____

_____

10.4.   Look at the indicators listed in Table 10–3 (p. 325). List the nations with the lowest and highest rates of literacy and per-capita energy consumption. Why are these indicators useful in comparing the level of development of nations? What do the figures on energy consumption tell us about the pitfalls in the measurement of development?

_____

_____

_____

_____

_____

_____

_____

_____

_____

_____

_____

_____

_____

_____

_____

_____

_____

_____

_____

_____

_____

NAME _____ **DATE** _____

10.5. How does nostalgia for the past explain why people often view social change as negative? Describe some changes that occurred in the last century that you believe were negative and others that you believe were positive. What does your list indicate about theories of social change as progress?

_____

_____

_____

_____

_____

_____

_____

_____

_____

_____

_____

_____

_____

_____

_____

_____

_____

_____

_____

_____

_____

_____

_____

_____

10.6. Look at Picasso's *Guernica* in the essay on Art and Social Change. What is the artist seeking to convey about the way civilians experience war and its effects on their society?

_____

_____

_____

_____

_____

_____

_____

_____

_____

_____

_____

_____

_____

_____

_____

_____

_____

_____

_____

_____

_____

CHAPTER 11

11.1.   What is meant by structural mobility? Do you think the large-scale reduction in manufacturing industries that has occurred in the United States results in structural mobility among blue-collar workers? Explain.

_____

_____

_____

_____

_____

_____

_____

_____

_____

_____

_____

_____

_____

_____

_____

_____

_____

_____

_____

_____

_____

_____

_____

11.2.   Youth magazines in the former Soviet Union contained stories about workers such as Tatyana, a loom operator in the big cotton mills of Uzbekistan. As a girl of eighteen she entered the mill and learned to run her loom very quickly. Soon she could run four looms, and before long she was setting records by operating six and then eight looms. She also became the head of her textile union branch and a party activist. What was the purpose of stories like this one?

_____

_____

_____

_____

_____

_____

_____

_____

_____

_____

_____

_____

_____

_____

_____

_____

_____

_____

NAME _____   **DATE** _____

11.3. Consider several individuals whom you know well, and think about how you conduct yourself with each of them—that is, your demeanor toward them. How does your demeanor express your feelings about the degree of deference that is due to you—or to the other person—in each case?

_____

_____

_____

_____

_____

_____

_____

_____

_____

_____

_____

_____

_____

_____

_____

_____

_____

_____

_____

_____

_____

_____

_____

_____

11.4.   Refer to Table 11.1 (p. 372). In which country did the largest percentage of sons with non-manual occupations have fathers with manual occupations?

_____

In which country did the largest percentage of sons with nonmanual occupations have fathers who were farmers?

_____

In which country was intergenerational mobility among manual workers lowest?

_____

11.5.   Do the events that have occurred in the former Soviet Union indicate that all attempts to ease the effects of inequalities of wealth and income are doomed to failure? Is the dream of a classless society a thing of the past, and if so, what does that imply for efforts to reduce disparities in income and wealth?

_____

_____

_____

_____

_____

_____

_____

_____

_____

_____

_____

_____

_____

_____

NAME _____   **DATE** _____

11.6. Look at the Visual Sociology section of Chapter 11. What social classes are depicted in these photos? In what ways are the people in these photos different from people you would normally encounter in your own society, especially in terms of the way their class position determines the course of their lives?

_____

_____

_____

_____

_____

_____

_____

_____

_____

_____

_____

_____

_____

_____

_____

_____

_____

_____

_____

_____

_____

CHAPTER 12

12.1. To what social class, if any, would you say you belong? Why ?

_____

_____

_____

_____

_____

_____

_____

_____

_____

_____

_____

_____

_____

_____

_____

_____

_____

_____

_____

_____

_____

_____

12.2.   The accompanying chart divides the total population of American families (66 million families) into fifths, or quintiles, each of which contains the same number of families (about 13 million). The highest quintile contains the families with the highest incomes (those earning $61,490 or more a year) and so on down to the lowest quintile (families earning $16,846 or less a year). On the right-hand side of the chart, draw boxes representing the proportion of total income earned by each quintile, connecting each box to the appropriate quintile. Use the following information:

Top quintile:	44.3 percent
Fourth quintile:	23.8 percent
Third quintile:	16.6 percent
Second quintile:	10.8 percent
Bottom quintile:	4.6 percent

What does the resulting chart indicate about the distribution of income in the United States?

Aggregate Family Income Distribution, by Quintiles, 1990

Top quintile
(families earning
$61,490 and over)

Fourth quintile
(families earning
$42,040–61,490)

Third quintile
(families earning
$29,044–42,040)

Second quintile
(families earning
$16,846–29,044

Bottom quintile
(families earning
$16,846 and under)

NAME _____   **DATE** _____

12.3.   As we travel along the nation's highways, we may see "ghost farms" amid what appears to be fertile farmland. Some of these ghost farms may be due to the construction of the highways, but far more are a result of structural changes affecting the traditional family farm. Explain.

_____

_____

_____

_____

_____

_____

_____

_____

_____

_____

_____

_____

_____

_____

_____

_____

_____

_____

_____

12.4.   The gap in educational attainment between blacks and whites has narrowed considerably in recent years. Do you think this change will affect the social-class position of the average black family in the near future? Why or why not?

_____

_____

_____

_____

_____

_____

_____

_____

_____

_____

_____

_____

_____

_____

_____

_____

_____

_____

_____

_____

_____

NAME _____ **DATE** _____

12.5. What reasons can you give to support the idea that education in the United States diminishes the strength of the class system? What reasons can you offer to support the argument that education contributes to the maintenance of the existing class system?

_____

_____

_____

_____

_____

_____

_____

_____

_____

_____

_____

_____

_____

_____

_____

_____

_____

_____

_____

_____

_____

_____

_____

_____

_____

12.6. The photo essay on diet and social class includes a picture of a woman buying bottled water. What details in the picture provide information about this woman's social-class position?

_____

_____

_____

_____

_____

_____

_____

_____

_____

_____

_____

_____

_____

_____

_____

_____

_____

_____

_____

_____

_____

_____

CHAPTER 13

13.1.   Your four grandparents probably represent one or more of the racial and ethnic groups whose members have immigrated to the United States in the last three centuries. What are those groups? Are any of them considered a minority group today?

_____

_____

_____

_____

_____

_____

_____

_____

_____

_____

_____

_____

_____

_____

_____

_____

_____

_____

_____

_____

_____

_____

_____

13.2.   Refer to Figure 13.1 (p. 431) and answer the following questions.

a. What is the largest immigrant group for which the number of people arriving in the United States peaked in 1980 or later?

_____

b. What was the largest immigrant group to arrive in the United States in the nineteenth century?

_____

c. Explain why the groups listed in this figure account for 85 percent of the total number of immigrants who have arrived since the nation's founding.

_____

13.3.   Do you see evidence of racial and/or ethnic stratification in your community? If so, describe the form it takes. Do you think the United States is a truly pluralistic society? Why or why not?

_____
_____
_____
_____
_____
_____
_____
_____
_____
_____
_____
_____
_____
_____
_____
_____
_____

NAME _____ **DATE** _____

13.4.   In *Tally's Corner*, his classic study of a group of black men, Elliot Liebow reports the following exchange: "In the middle of the discussion, Richard interrupted and nodded at me. 'Now Ellix here is white, as you can see, but he's one of my best friends. Him and me are real tight. You can say anything you want, right to his face. He's real nice.' 'Well,' said his Aunt Pearl, 'I always did say there are some nice white people.'"[1] What does this remark imply about the nature of prejudice?

_____

_____

_____

_____

_____

_____

_____

_____

_____

_____

_____

_____

_____

_____

_____

_____

_____

_____

_____

_____

_____

[1]Elliot Liebow, *Tally's Corner: A Study of Negro Streetcorner Men* (Boston: Little, Brown, 1967), p. 250.

13.5.   The subtleties of language are often more important in a political campaign than they generally are in everyday conversations among friends and family members. How does Ross Perot's address to the NAACP in 1992 illustrate this fact? If you and people close to you were addressed as "you people," would you be offended? Why are members of the NAACP prone to be especially sensitive about such a form of address by a presidential candidate?

_____

_____

_____

_____

_____

_____

_____

_____

_____

_____

_____

_____

_____

_____

_____

_____

_____

_____

_____

_____

_____

_____

_____

_____

NAME _____   DATE _____

13.6. Look at the Visual Sociology section of this chapter and at the one in Chapter 15, which also deals with gypsies. From what you see in both sets of photos, offer some possible explanations for why gypsies are often victims of discrimination and intergroup hostility.

_____

_____

_____

_____

_____

_____

_____

_____

_____

_____

_____

_____

_____

_____

_____

_____

_____

_____

_____

_____

_____

_____

_____

CHAPTER 14

14.1.   Refer to Figures 14–2 and 14–3 (pp. 470–471) and answer the following questions:

a. What percent of India's population is in the youngest age cohort?

_____

b. Who lives longer in advanced industrialized nations, males or females?

_____

c. How do the youngest age cohorts in third-world nations compare to those in advanced industrialized nations?

_____

14.2.   Describe your mother's work roles. If she is employed outside the home, in what occupation is she employed? Does her dual role create conflict in her life? Were you socialized to believe that certain roles are "natural" for men and women? Do you expect your husband/wife to perform specific roles?

_____

_____

_____

_____

_____

_____

_____

_____

_____

_____

_____

_____

_____

_____

14.3. Have you encountered sexism or ageism in your day-to-day life? If so, what form did it take?

_____

_____

_____

_____

_____

_____

_____

_____

_____

_____

_____

_____

_____

_____

_____

_____

_____

_____

_____

_____

_____

_____

_____

_____

NAME _____   **DATE** _____

14.4.   An article by Felice Schwartz in the *Harvard Business Review* ("Management Women and the New Facts of Life," January-February 1989) generated considerable controversy by suggesting that large companies should establish two career tracks for women: one for "career-primary" women and another for women who wish to combine a career with child rearing. The latter, dubbed the "Mommy track," would involve less career advancement but greater flexibility in terms of work hours, maternity leave, and the like. Critics of the idea argue that it would have the effect of keeping women who are both career- and family-oriented out of top management positions, while supporters say it would enable such women to enter management ranks to the extent that they are willing and able to do so. What is your opinion on this issue? Do you think there should be a "Daddy track"?

14.5. Which do you think is more problematic for societies, the demand by women for entry into previously all-male occupations such as those of police officer and combat soldier, or the persistent treatment of entire categories of people, such as women and the aged, in discriminatory ways? In your opinion, how should such problems be resolved in the future?

_____

_____

_____

_____

_____

_____

_____

_____

_____

_____

_____

_____

_____

_____

_____

_____

_____

_____

_____

_____

_____

_____

_____

_____

NAME _____   **DATE** _____

14.6.   Look at the Visual Sociology section of Chapter 14. What connections do you think Imogen Cunningham makes between the social situation of the people she photographs and their emotional well-being? Try to select details from the photographs that illustrate your argument.

_____

_____

_____

_____

_____

_____

_____

_____

_____

_____

_____

_____

_____

_____

_____

_____

_____

_____

_____

_____

_____

_____

_____

CHAPTER 15

15.1. When other institutions in a society change, families must adapt to those changes, and when the family changes, other institutions will be affected. Can you use the debate over the rights of gay and lesbian couples as an example? Can you think of other examples of each of these effects?

_____

_____

_____

_____

_____

_____

_____

_____

_____

_____

_____

_____

_____

_____

_____

_____

_____

_____

_____

_____

15.2.   Refer to Fgure 15–2 (p. 510) and draw a similar chart showing your own extended family.

NAME _____   **DATE** _____

15.3.   Consider several couples with whom you are acquainted. Do their relationships seem to support the theory of complementary needs? Do they support the theory of emotional reciprocity?

_____

_____

_____

_____

_____

_____

_____

_____

_____

_____

_____

_____

_____

_____

_____

_____

_____

_____

_____

_____

_____

_____

_____

15.4.   Several trends can be identified that are likely to affect the future of the family. Among them are the increasing proportion of women in the paid labor force, an increased tendency on the part of women to demand that household tasks be shared equally, greater acceptance of the desire of many fathers to spend more time with their children, a blurring of the distinctions between jobs considered appropriate for men and women, and other related trends. Can you see these trends at work in your community? If so, how are they affecting families with whom you are acquainted?

_____

_____

_____

_____

_____

_____

_____

_____

_____

_____

_____

_____

_____

_____

_____

_____

_____

_____

_____

_____

_____

NAME _____   **DATE** _____

15.5.   Although there is much debate about the changes occurring in family structure, Americans seem to resent politicians who claim to know what structure is best. Discuss this point with reference to the "family values" controversy that played a central part in the 1992 presidential election campaign.

_____

_____

_____

_____

_____

_____

_____

_____

_____

_____

_____

_____

_____

_____

_____

_____

_____

_____

_____

_____

_____

_____

15.6. The photo essay that accompanies this chapter includes a picture of several members of the Ivanovich family, some of whom were teenagers at the time the picture was taken. Do you think these young people are likely to remain within the extended family and maintain its values and life-ways? What do your conclusions suggest about the theory that extended families such as this one gradually cease to maintain their cohesiveness as a society becomes larger and more complex?

_____

_____

_____

_____

_____

_____

_____

_____

_____

_____

_____

_____

_____

_____

_____

_____

_____

_____

_____

_____

_____

CHAPTER 16

16.1.   Give an example of a situation in which the separation of religion from governmental and educational institutions has been challenged.

_____

_____

_____

_____

_____

_____

_____

_____

_____

_____

_____

_____

_____

_____

_____

_____

_____

_____

_____

_____

_____

16.2. Refer to Figure 16–3 (p. 563). In what areas of the United States are Lutherans concentrated? Latter Day Saints? Methodists?

_____

_____

_____

_____

_____

_____

_____

_____

_____

_____

_____

_____

_____

_____

_____

_____

_____

_____

_____

_____

_____

_____

_____

NAME _____   **DATE** _____

16.3.   At least 2000 followers of a religious group, the Church Universal and Triumphant, have paid up to $10,000 for a place in an elaborate system of underground shelters that the church has built in Livingston, Montana. Their leader, known as Guru Ma, has said that worldwide nuclear war is imminent. Nonmembers dismiss the shelters as a scam; members say they are harassed by outsiders. What factors might have contributed to the development of such a cult and to the attitudes of its members?

_____

_____

_____

_____

_____

_____

_____

_____

_____

_____

_____

_____

_____

_____

_____

_____

_____

_____

_____

_____

_____

_____

16.4. Describe the process of secularization, using examples, and explain how secularization helps account for the decline in the influence of organized religions during the past two centuries. Also indicate some of the limits of secularization, using examples of the continuing influence of organized religions in our society or others.

_____
_____
_____
_____
_____
_____
_____
_____
_____
_____
_____
_____
_____
_____
_____
_____
_____
_____
_____
_____
_____

NAME _____ **DATE** _____

16.5.   Why did Marx describe religion as "the opium of the masses"? How does the early history of Christianity offer a refutation of the Marxian view?

_____

_____

_____

_____

_____

_____

_____

_____

_____

_____

_____

_____

_____

_____

_____

_____

_____

_____

_____

_____

_____

_____

_____

_____

16.6.   The photo essay that accompanies this chapter includes a picture of a street preacher. What does this picture indicate about the nature of religious expression in this form of religious practice, in contrast to the picture of an Episcopalian church service?

_____

_____

_____

_____

_____

_____

_____

_____

_____

_____

_____

_____

_____

_____

_____

_____

_____

_____

_____

_____

_____

_____

_____

NAME _____ **DATE** _____

17.5. How is the promise of mobility through education compromised by inequalities in educational institutions? Use specific examples of inequalities and the population groups that are affected positively or negatively by those inequalities.

_____

_____

_____

_____

_____

_____

_____

_____

_____

_____

_____

_____

_____

_____

_____

_____

_____

_____

_____

_____

_____

_____

_____

_____

17.6.   Look at the picture of a student facing a tank in Tiananmen Square (Visual Sociology: Students and Social Change). What feelings does it evoke? Do you think the students' cause was hopeless from the beginning?

_____

_____

_____

_____

_____

_____

_____

_____

_____

_____

_____

_____

_____

_____

_____

_____

_____

_____

_____

_____

_____

_____

_____

_____

_____

_____

NAME _____   DATE _____

CHAPTER 18

18.1. In 1989 two economists, Jeff Biddle and Daniel Hamermesh, published the results of a study of why people sleep. They found that "sleep is, in part, a matter of economic discretion: People sleep less when time on the job is more valuable" (*New York Times*, August 2, 1989, p. A1). On the average, a wage increase of 25 percent reduces sleep time by about 1 percent; if a person's wages are doubled, that person will spend 20 minutes less in bed. Do you think this is an adequate explanation of why some people sleep more than others? What other factors might account for such differences?

_____
_____
_____
_____
_____
_____
_____
_____
_____
_____
_____
_____
_____
_____
_____
_____
_____
_____
_____
_____

18.2. "The bourgeoisie," wrote Marx and Engels in *The Communist Manifesto*, "by the rapid improvement of all instruments of production, by the immensely facilitated means of communication, draws all, even the most backward, nations into civilization . . . . It compels all nations, on pain of extinction, to adopt the bourgeois mode of production."[2] Do you think this statement accurately describes the modern world economic system? Why or why not?

---

[2]Karl Marx and Friedrich Engels, *The Communist Manifesto*, trans. Samuel Moore (New York: Washington Square Press, 1964/1848), p. 64.

18.3. Refer to Figure 18–2 (p. 627). For 1969 and 1989, calculate the difference between overall median earnings and the earnings of the four education categories. Show your results in a table, using a plus or a minus sign to indicate the direction of the difference.

18.4. The human relations approach to labor–management relations was developed from Elton Mayo's experiments, which showed that increased productivity could be obtained by emphasizing teamwork among workers and managers. Can you identify any flaws in this approach? If so, what are they?

_____

_____

_____

_____

_____

_____

_____

_____

_____

_____

_____

_____

_____

_____

_____

_____

_____

_____

_____

_____

_____

_____

NAME _____   **DATE** _____

18.5.   The famous sign in the Clinton campaign headquarters, "The Economy, Stupid," represented a great difference in thinking between the Reagan–Bush philosophy of laissez-faire and Clinton's liberal-democratic call for intervention to stimulate the economy and reduce the federal government's budget deficit. Explain the differences between the two views and how they translate into the kinds of policies advocated by each side in the 1992 presidential election campaign.

_____

_____

_____

_____

_____

_____

_____

_____

_____

_____

_____

_____

_____

_____

_____

_____

_____

_____

_____

_____

18.6. "What's in a name?" In corporate America, great importance is attached to corporate and product names. Use examples from the Visual Sociology section of the chapter to discuss this point.

_____

_____

_____

_____

_____

_____

_____

_____

_____

_____

_____

_____

_____

_____

_____

_____

_____

_____

_____

_____

_____

_____

_____

_____

CHAPTER 19

19.1.   Why did Max Weber describe politics as "the slow boring of hard boards"?

_____

_____

_____

_____

_____

_____

_____

_____

_____

_____

_____

_____

_____

_____

_____

_____

_____

_____

_____

_____

_____

_____

_____

_____

19.2.   Glance at your daily newspaper. You will probably see at least one article about a country that is undergoing a major political upheaval or "crisis of legitimacy." What is the nature of the crisis?

_____

_____

_____

_____

_____

_____

_____

_____

_____

_____

_____

_____

_____

_____

_____

_____

_____

_____

_____

_____

_____

_____

_____

NAME _____   **DATE** _____

19.3.   Refer to Table 19–3 (p. 667). According to the table, the greatest gap between European stable democracies and Latin American stable dictatorships is in which of the following areas?

_____   literacy rates

_____   per-capita income

_____   energy consumption per capita

_____   percent of population living in cities with more than 100,000 inhabitants

19.4.   In *The Power Elite*, C. Wright Mills wrote that the private decisions of corporate executives "determine the size and shape of the national economy, the level of employment, the purchasing power of the consumer, the prices that are advertised, the investments that are channeled." As a result, he continued, they "govern at many of the vital points of everyday life in America, and no powers effectively and consistently countervail against them."[1] Do you think the power of corporate executives constitutes a threat to democratic political institutions? Why or why not?

_____

_____

_____

_____

_____

_____

_____

_____

_____

_____

_____

_____

_____

_____

_____

_____

[1]C. Wright Mills, *The Power Elite* (New York: Oxford University Press, 1956), p. 125.

19.5. Show how politics makes a difference in your life, either positively or negatively or both. Use specific examples of laws or politics that influence your behavior or might influence you in the future.

_____

_____

_____

_____

_____

_____

_____

_____

_____

_____

_____

_____

_____

_____

_____

_____

_____

_____

_____

_____

_____

_____

_____

_____

NAME _____   DATE _____

19.6.   Consider the picture of the police officer with an attack dog in the photo essay that accompanies this chapter. What does this picture indicate about the difficulty of establishing the institution of free and fair elections in a society?

_____

_____

_____

_____

_____

_____

_____

_____

_____

_____

_____

_____

_____

_____

_____

_____

_____

_____

_____

_____

_____

_____

_____

_____

20.2. Give an example of a recent technological advance that has had both positive and negative effects. Do you see evidence that policymakers in government or business are attempting to alleviate the negative impacts of that particular technology?

_____

_____

_____

_____

_____

_____

_____

_____

_____

_____

_____

_____

_____

_____

_____

_____

_____

_____

_____

_____

_____

_____

_____

NAME _____ **DATE** _____

20.3. In what ways does medical technology illustrate the interactions between technology and other aspects of the social order?

_____

_____

_____

_____

_____

_____

_____

_____

_____

_____

_____

_____

_____

_____

_____

_____

_____

_____

_____

_____

_____

_____

20.4. In April 1990 the long-heralded Hubble space telescope, designed to view the heavens from orbit 380 miles above the earth, was launched. Within two months, scientists discovered that the $1.5 billion telescope contained a serious flaw—a spherical aberration in one of its mirrors—making it one of the most spectacular failures in the history of technology. Drawing upon what you have read about the dimensions of technology, comment on the possible reasons for the Hubble fiasco.

NAME _____   **DATE** _____

20.5. How does techno-fix thinking influence the way people feel about environmental crises? Use specific examples of environmental concerns and the technological changes associated with them. Why is there growing disillusionment with technological solutions to complex social and environmental problems?

_____

_____

_____

_____

_____

_____

_____

_____

_____

_____

_____

_____

_____

_____

_____

_____

_____

_____

_____

_____

_____

_____

_____

_____

_____

20.6.   Look at the picture of the Three Mile Island nuclear-power plant in the Visual Sociology section of this chapter. What feelings does it evoke? Would you continue to live in your hometown if such a plant were built there? Is it realistic to call for a return to simpler energy sources based on "the warm power of the sun"?